Crazy Faith, Unexplainable Peace

A LESSON MY MOTHER TAUGHT ME

ROMONA JACKSON

Crazy Faith, Unexplainable Peace. Copyright 2022 by Romona Jackson. All rights reserved. No part of this publication may be reproduced, distributed, or transmitted in any form or by any means, including photocopying, recording, or other electronic or mechanical methods, without the prior written permission of the publisher, except in the case of brief quotations embodied in critical reviews and certain other noncommercial uses permitted by copyright law.

For permission requests, write to the publisher, addressed "Attention: Permissions Coordinator," 205 N. Michigan Avenue, Suite #810, Chicago, IL 60601. 13th & Joan books may be purchased for educational, business or sales promotional use. For information, please email the Sales Department at sales@13thandjoan.com.

Printed in the U. S. A.

First Printing, July 2022.

Library of Congress Cataloging-in-Publication Data has been applied for.

ISBN: 978-1-7322479-8-7

For you Mommy

As I read "Crazy Faith: Unexplainable Peace", one word repeated over and over in my head: perspective.

I watched Romona walk through one of the toughest times she will ever face with quiet grace and dignity. She never let what was happening with her Mother impact her interactions with others. She always had a kind word and ready prayer for those that were struggling without bringing attention to her situation. While I never had the opportunity to meet Mrs. Jackson, I felt I knew her through my conversations with Romona. Through the daily choice to believe in God's plan and her "Crazy Faith", Romona made it through to the other side stronger than she realized. Every day we are faced with challenges and hardships that we can choose to let tear us down or face them with faith and courage.

Romona, choosing to share your journey with all of the love and pain, that is so deeply personal, with the world is an extremely courageous act of love and "Crazy Faith". "For I know the plans I have for you," declares the Lord, "plans to prosper you and not to harm you, plans to give you hope and a future." - Jeremiah 29:11

Michelle Marvin

God puts things in our path at just the right moment. You had no idea how much I needed to read your book and hear your message right now. It was hard to read, as you know I lost my mother, my best friend, 7 months before you lost yours. My vision was blurred with tears several times. Through your words, I was reminded of all the beautiful memories I have of her. I needed to hear your message about self care and self love. Things I knew but had lost focus on. You also reminded me of the importance of having faith and through that finding peace. It was a beautiful book that truly connected with my heart. Thank you so much for sharing it with me.

Ruth Hull

"Crazy Faith Unexplainable Peace: A lesson my mother taught me" is a heartwarming book about an incredibly special relationship between a Daughter and a Mother and the role faith had in their journey. Each page leaves you pondering who was teaching who what as their incredible story unfolds and life lessons prevail. It leaves you remembering what the most important thing in this crazy thing we call life is and leaves you longing to make the adjustments you need in your own life to get there. It gives you permission to act and reminds you that you are truly in control of you own story. This book provides you the space and time to digest the words and put them to work in the way that is most meaningful to you vs a quick read that ends up collecting dust on a shelf. In a world and an era where it can be easy to lose yourself and lose faith Romona brings a sense of hope and peace to it all.

Sheena Tapia

The moment I started reading Romona's book "Crazy Faith", I was hooked because not only have I seen her walk in the Lord, but I've also watched her match her walk with her faith. The fact that she never complained about the sickness and transition of her mother into the arms of Jesus is a testament to that faith. Yet it was not only Crazy Faith but a walk in God's Perfect Peace. At times, I have struggled with the spiritual meaning of Isaiah 26:3-4, but Romona is a shining example to me of these Scriptures and through her insight and experience, I found clarity, Perfect Peace, and crazy faith in these scriptures when my own mother transitioned to her Heavenly Home this year as well. (July 9, 2021). This book is a must-read for anyone that has lost a loved one because God chose a vessel like Romona to go through a state of brokenness to show readers like you and me that His grace is sufficient, and His strength is made perfect in brokenness to heal any emotional pain. We all know that most families go through some type of drama, and I commend Romona for her courage to share her pain and struggle and allow us into her life and walk with God.

Elder Terry J. Robinson Sr.

Readers will be able to enter into their own thoughts and moments when they read. As I read, I felt all the feels, smiled, chuckled and got a little mad. "This book will meet people and invite them in but challenge them to be and love better."

Dr. Latisha Reeves- Henry

Your mom's soul is smiling! This is a beautiful tribute to her not only as the wonderful mother she was but also the strong woman she was!!! This shows us all no matter what we've been through, every day is another chance to grow, change and be a better version of ourselves.

Terren Grimble

The Journey Chronicled

Foreword Crazy Faith 1

Introduction 4

Chapter 72 "Your Wings were ready, but my Heart was not!" 9

Just to Know Us! 20

Life Lesson: "Do Something Good for Yourself!" 30

Life Lesson: "Don't Take No Wooden Nickels" (Self-Love) ... 44

A Test of Faith 73

Unexplainable Peace: A Hole Where She Used To Be 86

The Journey Ends, Legacy Begins 94

Praise God No Matter What 100

Acknowledgments 115

About the Author 117

Foreword

Crazy Faith

December 22, 2010, was a typical morning. Since we were just a few days out from Christmas, my husband and I talked about the gifts we needed to finish buying for family and friends while we got dressed for work. He walked down the hall to get our then eight-month-old son ready to head to daycare while I finished getting ready for the Board Meeting that I had first thing that morning. But something wasn't right. I felt off. I was having strange cramping sensations while zipping up my dress when I suddenly felt something wet trickle down my leg. I was five months pregnant with our second son, a surprise pregnancy, and knew the water leaking could only be amniotic fluid. "No," I said under my breath. "Not again."

On February 9, 2010, my oldest son was born at twenty-six weeks. He was 2 lbs. 9 oz and three and a half months too early. He stayed in the neonatal intensive care unit for almost four months after he was born, fighting for his life. He almost died twice, and the psychological trauma was still fresh. With him, a similar morning signaled something was wrong. Cramping and leaking fluid. I told my husband I had to go to the hospital, then I emailed the Board Chair and told her I wouldn't be at the meeting. I emailed my report, then climbed in my car and drove to North Florida Regional Medical Center.

When my husband arrived after taking our baby to daycare, the doctor delivered the news we didn't want to hear. "Your water broke, Mrs. Jones," the doctor said. "You have no more amniotic fluid, and your pregnancy is no longer viable." My world stopped spinning, and my heart sank. "What are our options," I asked, already knowing the answer? "There are none," she said. "I'm so sorry. You're going to deliver your baby, but his lungs aren't formed, so he won't be able to breathe." I let out a guttural cry as all of the strength I had left my body. My sweet baby, Daniel, would be born… to die.

My husband and I prayed to God for a miracle. We asked God to show forth his power. We asked close friends and family to pray with us for a miracle. We believed it would happen. Even if I had to lay in bed for the next four months, I was willing to do it if that meant Daniel could live. But at 7:33pm that night, Daniel entered the world, and my husband and I held him in a too-large blanket until his tiny chest stopped rising and fell for the last time. My faith failed. My prayers failed. My hope failed. My God failed. Or did they?

The morning after delivering my baby, I walked out of the hospital with a still-pregnant appearing belly, only to find a teenage girl leaning against the wall with a large belly still filled with a baby… smoking a cigarette. Had it not been for the unexplainable peace of God, I probably would have been locked up for assaulting that girl out of anger, but instead, I simply noticed it and kept walking. When I got home, I crawled into my bed and slept for hours, and when I woke up, my baby boy TJ was smiling and laughing as he zoomed around the house in his walker. At that moment, I heard God say, "I work all things together for your good, Nona. That doesn't mean everything we feel good; it just means it will become good. I promise you."

When it seems like our faith, prayers, hope, and even God himself have forsaken us, we must learn to lean on who God *is* when we can't find comfort in what God *does*. True, God is sovereign, and he could raise the dead, heal the sick and cause the blind to see. But, even if he doesn't, he is *still* good because God's character doesn't change. God doesn't just give us peace. He gives us himself because he *is* peace. When the pain of life makes you question God, never forget that he is faithful to his word, and he works all things together for our good.

After losing Daniel, we learned why my oldest son was born prematurely. And, through a simple, painless procedure, I was able to carry my youngest son to term. He was born healthy, happy, and full of life at almost nine pounds. You will be encouraged by Romona's story because, like me, God has given her beauty in the ashes of her pain. And the beauty he has given her is manifested on these pages. She is a gift, and her story is a treasure for us all because, when you lose the thing you want the most, you can still retain the peace of God.

Praying God's peace and healing upon you as you read. It's time for a return to crazy faith.

Introduction

You may ask what is "Crazy Faith and Unexplainable Peace" my answer is my invitation to each of you, inside of the journey that changed my life forever. When my Mother, Carolyn Ruth White Jackson, gained her wings, I was devastated. However, I learned so much as I watched her fight a battle in which she won the ultimate victory. I was determined to believe God for my Mother's healing on this side despite what others would tell me, and regardless of what I saw, Crazy Faith! I chose to believe in God until the situation came to a close. I am reminded of King David, who fasted and prayed, wept, and lamented over his dying son, believing God for a miracle until his Son passed away. He then got up, cleaned himself up, stopped his weeping, and ate a good meal, to the disbelief of his servants. They wondered why he was calm, cool, and collected. Proverbially speaking, when his son died, they were expecting him to be torn apart as he was while his son was sick…..This is called Unexplainable Peace.

I watched my mother's journey on this side, which I now call it her labor which began on April 21, 2020, up until she received her reward on October 24, 2021, at 12:37am. I learned so much that I want to share it with you in hopes that it will inspire and encourage someone, just as it did for me. I endeavor to unfold valuable life lessons, connected with what God has to say about those lessons, to help chronicle the true love of a Mother and a daughter. This book will not be for everyone, but for those it resonates with. I pray that you receive all that God intended for you to receive. He is the Author, holding the pen. I am just the vessel He chose to use.

Dear Mommy,

As I sit and write this letter, I still cannot believe I am writing a letter that you will never physically read. I always dreamed of us growing old together, just you and me. If anyone had told me that you wouldn't be here, I would have literally fought them and repented later. When I say you were my world on Earth, you were. You were my everything. I used to pray daily that God would restore all of the years that you endured hardship because all I wanted to do was see you smile. I still wake up almost two years later, having to remind myself that you are not here with me. I miss your voice, hearing you call me "Baby-girl." I miss the way you laughed, I miss seeing you walk, I miss kissing your forehead, I miss the way you used to scream when I surprised you, and I miss how appreciative you were for all that you received. I miss when you call and how your picture would pop up on my phone. We started every conversation with 'Hey Beautiful,' and you would say 'No, You are the beautiful one,' and I replied because

I got it from my mommita! You loved pictures and were ready to pose at a moment's notice. Mommy, I miss you. I never understood a mother's love. No one will ever pray for me, love me, support me like you.

I am going through so much, the good outweighs the bad, and I know you are here with me. I am smiling and pressing through only by His Strength and His Grace because I know that He does not make mistakes, and you would want me to be strong. I never fathomed you not being here with me. I didn't want to see you go, but God chose differently. Now I am here striving to live out the legacy you left. Striving to make you proud, so when God allows you to look upon me, you will love what you see from Heaven's balcony. This hurt will never go away, but daily, God helps it to subside a little more so that it gets easier to bear! I am blessed beyond measure to have had you as my mom, to teach me, mold me and shape me just by the way you lived your life. We laughed, we cried, we argued, but we loved hard, and the love we had, no one would ever be able to comprehend. I bless God for allowing me to witness what having a good, God-fearing Proverbs 31 Mother looks like and for giving me the desire to carry forth your example by the life I live. I love you, mommy, miss you, and pray that I always make you proud!

Until we meet again,

Your Baby-girl

PROVERBS 31:10-31 (THE MESSAGE)

A good woman is hard to find and worth far more than diamonds.
Her husband trusts her without reserve and never has reason to regret it.
Never spiteful, she treats him generously all her life long.
She shops around for the best yarns and cotton and enjoys knitting and sewing.
She's like a trading ship that sails to faraway places and brings back exotic surprises.
She's up before dawn, preparing breakfast for her family and organizing her day.
She looks over a field and buys it, then, with money she's put aside, plants a garden.
First thing in the morning, she dresses for work, rolls up her sleeves, eager to get started.
She senses the worth of her work and is in no hurry to call it quits for the day.
She's skilled in the crafts of home and hearth, diligent in homemaking.
She's quick to assist anyone in need and reaches out to help the poor.
She doesn't worry about her family when it snows; their winter clothes are all mended and ready to wear. She makes her own clothing and dresses in colorful linens and silks.

*Her husband is greatly respected when he deliberates
     with the city fathers.*
She designs gowns and sells them, brings the sweaters she knits to the dress shops.
*Her clothes are well-made and elegant, and she
     always faces tomorrow with a smile.*
*When she speaks, she has something worthwhile to
     say, and she always says it kindly.*
*She keeps an eye on everyone in her household and keeps
     them all busy and productive.*
*Her children respect and bless her; her husband joins
     in with words of praise:*
*"Many women have done wonderful things, but
     you've outclassed them all!"*
*Charm can mislead, and beauty soon fades. The
     woman to be admired and praised*
*is the woman who lives in the Fear-of-God. Give her
     everything she deserves!*
Adorn her life with praises!

Chapter 72

"Your Wings were ready, but my Heart was not!"

My mom never liked going to the doctor. She always said that when it was time for her to go to a doctor, the Lord would let her know, and she would not hesitate to go. Looking back, I believe it was because of her background within the medical field. She worked in hospitals and emergency rooms, and she was also a Certified Nursing Assistant, so she saw a lot which helped to erode her trust in doctors.

She had pain in her lower back. Although my mother was only 5'5, her stature did not fully contain all of who she was. She was beautifully caramel-colored and wore a short afro. She had strong arms, which helped her to carry the heavy loads she had to bear both physically and emotionally. But it was her smile for me. It would light up any room and change the atmosphere because when she smiled, it was so genuine that it caused her eyes to dance gracefully. But when the pain would come, it would wipe away all that strength for what seemed to be an eternity. Regardless, I hated it. I realize that hate is a strong word, but

I really hated it when my mom was under the weather. I couldn't stand for her to get a cold, and I heard how miserable it made her. She was such a good person. I never wanted her to experience pain. The pain, however, became unbearable, so she had to seek medical attention. They ran a battery of tests that showed that her left kidney was deformed, non-functioning. Her right kidney was doing all the work. This really helped to put into perspective for me how a person truly can survive with one kidney. My mother had been going for years with this, and we were none the wiser.

The test results revealed a blockage in her kidney, which turned out to be malignant. MALIGNANT, that word still haunts me! MALIGNANT and next to that you put MY MOTHER. Then it hit like a ton of bricks. My Mother has cancer! As a family, we all were in shock but also in denial. We went into prayer mode and declared her healing and prayed that God's Hand would intervene, remove the cancer, and when she went back to the doctor, he would not find a trace of that horrible, debilitating disease within the body of the woman I called my Angel. My mom was strong, though! I could see the worry in her eyes. Her dark eyes, that slanted when she smiled, were truly open windows, that if you peered inside, you could see her every emotion in them, but you could also feel the love and the care that she carried on the inside of her soul in just one glimpse. She worried, but she still trusted and carried on. She encouraged us more than we encouraged her, it seems. But she had a resiliency that would not be defeated and a foundation that could not be rocked. She had hope and trust that helped her even when she did not know what tomorrow may bring. All I remember her saying was, *"kidney cancer?" "How? Who in the family had that type of cancer?" " I would have never thought I would get kidney cancer."* I still remember sitting and watching her as she asked this question. Although it was rhetorical, she asked, looking for an answer that could not be provided, or at least not by any of us. She would frown her face as she asked the questions, flailing her hands, then she would sit back, and a look of calm would take the place of the frowns, and she would say, *"I don't know, but I trust God!"*

As a family, we did all we could! We fasted, prayed, cried, yelled, screamed in anguish, but the fact still remained. Those ominous words scrolled across my mind like a marquee, MY MOTHER HAS CANCER! She had to have surgery. This scared the life out of me! You have to understand my mother was my Shero. I saw her endure knocks, kicks, and bruises and stand strong with each one. This? This hit differently! They scheduled the surgery for April 21, 2020, and unbeknownst to all of us, our lives were never going to be the same again.

The pandemic was in full force, so no one could be with my mom. So the family gathered the day before her surgery, and we prayed. I had heard my mom pray before, but the sound was different this time. My mom went around and hugged my aunts, my cousin, and then me. An eerie feeling overtook my body that I could not shake when she hugged me. I felt an emptiness like something was going to happen. I tried my best to shake it off. I didn't tell anyone. I just chalked it up to nervousness and the inability to be by her side. On the day of her surgery, we all sat outside of the hospital, waiting to hear from the doctor and praying for the best. After several hours, they came and said it was successful, and we all let out a shout of praise. The hard part was over, now, she must heal.

It took five long days for my mom to be released on April 26, 2021. When she was discharged, it was the best day ever. She came home, and now it was our turn to take care of the one who took care of us so unselfishly. We did everything we could to wait on her hand and foot, but that was not my mom's style. I smile as I remember. One morning, she sat in my Dad's recliner chair, which sits directly in front of the television. You know everyone has that special chair in the house that belongs to them, that no one dares to sit in because it has taken on their form! Well, this was the only chair my mom could sit in and find relief as she healed from surgery. As I came into the living room and looked at her, she was looking down. My father was in a mood, as he always was, and wasn't speaking to anyone. My mom coined it the "full moon" effect. He would be okay for one moment, and then the next, he was angry. People made him angry, conversations would make him angry, and people on the job made him angry. However, he never dealt with the root cause of the issue. He always brought his issues home. My mom felt the brunt of it all, and I just felt the residue. I remember going almost three months without hearing from my dad. That was just his nature. It was a battle between him and me when it came to my mother. It almost felt like a competition, so there was a lot of tension between us, and this really upset my mother. She wanted to talk, but my father refused, and this infuriated me! My mother said something I would never forget. She said, **"Mona, do you realize that I can die if my other kidney does work like it should?"**

My mom was one whom I coined as an overthinker. When she sat, she would think, and at times that could be scary (lol). If there were things going on with the family, or if she was trying to figure out things financially, she would run many scenarios through her mind, a series of what-ifs. She would often call and say, *"Mona, let me run something by you?"* or *"Mona, what do you think about this?"* or *"Mona, was I wrong for saying this?"* If she was planning to go on a trip, she would start packing three months ahead of time, because she didn't want to forget anything! (lol) I remember her preparing to go to Jerusalem. I would visit, and she had her suitcase open on the bed with outfits and toiletries pressed and nicely packed. She started shopping for Thanksgiving in August, buying little by little, catching things on sale, storing them away neatly, and when the time came, she was always more than prepared.

My mom was also very leery and skeptical because she had suffered through a lot of disappointments. So because she thought so much, she would often say, *"I am not going to be excited about anything until it happens!"* This was a trait that I picked up that I had to pray to release because this mindset will always have you in a state of fear. It will cause you to live in a constant state of "waiting for the other shoe to drop," so you never enjoy the fullness of the journey. I woke up one morning after she came home from the hospital and found her sitting in the recliner just thinking. The doctors told her everything was fine, they removed all of the cancer, but she had to go back and make sure that her right kidney was producing at the right levels. She heard, she knew, but I believe this morning was the morning my mom was trying to get us ready for life without her. She was facing her mortality and wanted us to face it too.

I called my father in. My father stands about 5'8 or 5'9. I inherited my chocolate complexion from him! He is stocky in build but always wears a stern face. I used to try to rub the frown lines from his forehead, but they were a permanent fixture! He reluctantly came in with a staunch attitude sealed with a look that said, "I am not what you want!" When my mother began to speak, he made it all about him and didn't want to hear anything she had to say. Before I knew it, I was screaming at the top of my lungs because I heard the hurt in my mom's voice, and for the first time ever, I saw her weak. My extremely overprotective nature regarding my mother kicked into overdrive and every bit of anger and disgust that I harbored over the years came out. I spewed every bit of it at him. I didn't care that he was my father. I didn't care about the impending consequences of my actions. I wanted him to feel all the years of anger that I had. The anger I carried because there was always yelling in the home, arguing in the home, throughout my childhood and right up until that day. I was angry that he didn't see that life was short. That we were coming to a crossroad that we never thought we would face. He was angry because he was feeling disrespected. That I had the audacity to yell and get toe to toe with him. He was angry because he felt he was bearing the burden of my mother's illness all alone. He was angry at the fact that his wife of fifty years was sick and he was helpless. He was there every day, when no one, especially me, was there. We stood at the forefront, yelling at the top of our lungs, while my mother stood silently, helpless. Words flew back and forth. The pressure became too much. It became physical. All I remember is my mom, shorter than us both and still weak, standing in between us with her medical bags and my father telling me to pack my bags and *get out*. The following day…I left.

It had been several weeks after what I would call the "debacle" since I left my parent's home. I communicated with my mom over the phone, video chat, and things of that nature, but all the while, my mom's health was taking a turn. We didn't know. My father and I were not speaking, which was, looking back, awful because so much time was wasted. I remember my father calling and leaving me a message that forever changed the way I looked at him. I remember finishing a five-mile run and walking up to my door, and I listened to the voicemail that said, *"for as long as you live, stay away from me!"* I look back now and replay the words that were many, but I know that it stemmed from pain. He felt like I didn't care that I did nothing, but he had no clue and always had a one-sided view that always reflected the words, deeds, and actions of the other person and never reflected the role he played. However, as time moved on, I had to move past those things, ask God to forgive me, ask him for forgiveness, and place Mona on the back burner so I could be there for my mom because that is all that mattered!

To fast forward, I vividly remember, and I believe this will be something that I will never forget. I traveled back and forth from Gainesville to be with my mom during her illness, she was non - responsive, but every day I went anyway. I would pray that I would walk in and see her sitting up and talking. I actually would have been happy if I walked in and she looked at me. October 24th felt different, and I didn't know why….it just did.

A week before, a palliative doctor came in to talk to my father and me about my mom's condition. She spoke of her not seeing my mom yet in the active stage of dying, but her condition is not getting better. I didn't quite know what a palliative doctor was, so I googled, of course, and found out it was a form of hospice. My heart sank. You see, I was avoiding talking to a hospice doctor. Hospice represented death to me, and I wasn't quite ready to have the discussion, well, at least not at that moment. She proceeded with the conversation and then pulled out this bright yellow form...bold letters on the top....**DO NOT RESUSCITATE**. She explained that because my mother is in an extremely weakened state, with no signs of getting better, she recommended that we sign the DNR and not put my mother through unnecessary pain, which only prolonged the inevitable. I wasn't in denial, but I also knew my mother was still living in the other room, and the thought of me preparing for her death I couldn't fathom.

Realists would say, Romona, snap out of it! Grow up! Instead, I lost it and told the doctor to get that paper out of my face. I am not ready to sign anything. I was literally hysterical. My father worked to calm me down and told the doctor we would discuss it later. I went back to sit with mom while my father left to grab a bite. My mother's oxygen wouldn't regulate no matter what they tried, then she had a rattling in her chest that she was too weak to clear…..I didn't know what was happening … .but God knew. They moved mom to a larger room with more gadgets to get her levels up. They only had to move her two doors down, but it was the worst experience ever, and I was there alone with the nurses.

My mom couldn't breathe, and she let out these screams that I will never forget as she frantically tried to grasp for air. They tried everything. I had to turn away so as to not see, but I could still hear, and my heart broke into a billion pieces. I turned to my mom only to find her looking right at me as she screamed. Mind you, my mom had not looked at me in weeks, and I broke. I went to her and began to whisper in her ear, *"it's okay, mommy," "it's okay, mommy,"* rubbing her back, her face, *"I'm here, mommy," "I am here."* Kissing her face, *"I got you"*…….God intervened, and they found something that worked. Her oxygen slowly began to regulate, and she calmed…..

Something still was not right. The night continued to move on as we sat with mom. It was time for the nurses' shift to change, and the nurse said, *"I will see you on Monday,"* but added five words that stung, *"...if you are still here."* I said to myself *if we are still here, what do you mean if?* They came to change my mom and give her meds, and as they handled my mom, she was almost lifeless. Her eyes were open, but the light within them...they were dim. They had to keep changing her. Another nurse came in and commented, *are you changing her again? They* responded *yes,* and she looked, turned, and left the room. She knew. They all knew. They finally finished and left us alone. I went over to my mom and sang "The Blood" in her ear. This was her favorite hymn, and no matter what, she always enjoyed hearing me sing this song, and she yelled and cried each time as if it was the first. I rubbed her soft skin on her face. Her face didn't have any signs of pain, just peace. I held her hands, kissed her fingers, and rubbed her head.

As we prepared to turn in, my dad turned the light off. No less than five minutes, I watched the monitor as her oxygen level remained high, but another number slowly declined…...her heart rate. I went into sheer panic, screaming for the call button for the nurse, yelling, **"HER HEART RATE IS DROPPING!"**, **"HER HEART RATE IS DROPPING! DO SOMETHING!"** The nurses came and stood by her bed. I couldn't believe my eyes. I couldn't believe what was happening as everyone else stood around watching. **"DO SOMETHING, DON'T JUST STAND THERE!**….. I didn't know then, but earlier that afternoon, my father signed the DNR form without telling me. I am sure knowing this fact would not have made this moment any easier, but I would have understood why they just stood around her, doing nothing. I fell to the floor and looked at the monitor, seventy-two.

That's when I stopped looking at the machine and watched my father holding her head. Then I watched the oxygen bag until it stopped thirty-seven minutes after midnight on October 24, 2020. My mom left me. My best friend in the universe left me here alone, and I felt empty, lifeless, and numb. I ran out of the room, with no shoes, trying to escape, and I never went back in. A nurse found me and sat on the cold floor with me, holding me as my world literally stopped spinning. My best friend, a confidante, Shero, left me….I picked up the phone and made two calls, one to my aunt and one to a friend. All I could utter was….*she's gone.* I was dazed and prayed someone would wake me up. I walked to the waiting room, pulled up two chairs, and laid down. I tried to get as small as I could, to disappear as the final moments replayed over and over like a bad movie.

A million thoughts run through your mind, enough to plunge you deeper into an abyss of darkness without any hope of seeing the light. I couldn't go back into the room. I watched family members come in and walk to the room, but I couldn't bring myself to go back to see such a beautiful life now…...lifeless. Going back into the room meant I had to accept it. It meant its finality, and I wasn't ready to face the FINAL.

> *The Blood that Jesus shed for me*
> *Way back on Calvary*
> *The Blood that gives me my strength*
> *From day to day*
> *It will never lose Its Power*
> *For It reaches to the highest mountain*
> *And It flows to the lowest valley*
> *Oh yes! The Blood*

ROMONA JACKSON

That gives me my strength
From day to day
It will never lose Its Power!

Just to Know Us!

*"Love is patient and kind; love does not envy or boast;
it is not arrogant or rude. It does not insist on its own
way, it is not irritable or resentful, it does not rejoice at
wrongdoing but rejoices with the truth.
Love bears all things, believes all things,
hopes all things, endures all things."*
– 1 Corinthians 13:4-7

My mother and I had a very unique relationship that evolved in such a special way. It is funny how the pressures of life will cause you to adapt in ways that you never thought possible. I was her only child, and from the start, we were best friends. She was one whom I would just watch and admire. I do not think she ever knew that until I got older. I admired her from the start and just would watch her all the time. She was my Shero, my perfect example of the Proverbs 31 woman. She didn't say a lot when I was growing up. Affection was not one of her strong suits, as she often admitted to me. Still, the way she showed her love was priceless, and I know that is what instilled in me so much affection for her and for others.

Breathe in...do you smell that? Sweet memories of delicious aromas coming from the kitchen are flooding my mind right now and making my mouth water! Carolyn Ruth was an EXCELLENT cook, and because of it, I had to shop in the HUSKY department, YES! a girl, shopping in the HUSKY department, I never knew such a thing as a husky existed. I mean husky? The name, in and of itself, was totally embarrassing! We had to go to the BASEMENT to get my clothes, no frilly skirts, and tops for me! It was all rugged and masculine. All through school and many phases of life, I battled with weight. I mean, who could resist, homemade biscuits with Aunt Jemima syrup? You couldn't just have one. My mom could also put some stuff together. She would make spaghetti with loads of hamburger meat. REAL spaghetti now, not the kind you pour the sauce on top! Nooo! The kind you cooked all together in one huge pot, and it burned a little at the bottom because it was so full. I called that the crust (lol). Then she would cook fried chicken and biscuits or cornbread. C'mon now! I was a porker. My plates, growing up, would go toe to toe with my father's plates. You couldn't tell the difference!

That's why Thanksgiving was so momentous!. It was my mom's favorite holiday. It was the main event to top all events. You dare not miss it. I think I only missed one and lived to tell the story. I cannot remember a small Thanksgiving. From the time when I sat at the kid's table, all the way to when I graduated to the grown-up table, we always had huge gatherings. Cooking together was our favorite pastime! It was what made our bonding time so special! She started me out by learning to peel the potatoes (my fingers are still traumatized from trying not to cut all the "meat" off of the potatoes!), then snapping the green beans and shelling the peas. If I accomplished the task, then I was rewarded by being able to lick the mixing spoon and the bowl when she finished her cake batter and sweet potato pie mix. Yes, this added even more to my huskiness (lol). Then as I got older, I moved on to cooking more, we divided the kitchen into two, and I cooked one half, and she cooked the other. One Thanksgiving, my mother's knee was broken, and she couldn't really walk or stand for long periods! I told her, "Coach, put me in!" and did she put me in! I cooked ninety percent of the meal, and no one could tell the difference in who cooked what. MISSION ACCOMPLISHED!

My mother was a *LADY*! I always believed there was a difference between being called a woman and being called a lady. As I explored this more, I found that the term lady carried a connotation of respect, the same as when you call a man a gentleman. To this day, I strive to be seen as a lady and not just a woman because of the respect I have for myself and the manner in which I carry myself. My mother, the Lady, dressed beautifully. Everything had to match. When she bought shoes, she bought the purse to match. She kept all of her shoes in their original boxes, her purses in plastic bags, and her jewelry all nicely ordered and placed in a beautiful jewelry box. I remember the first jewelry box she ever brought me. I can see it and hear it like it was yesterday. It was small and white with gold accent lines all around. When you opened it, a velvety pink fabric was on the inside. A small ballerina was placed in the center, on a round pedestal that turned. As you opened the lid, she danced, with her arms reaching to the heavens while twirling on one foot as the music played. My mom bought me a necklace and a ring, and those were the first additions to my jewelry box. I was so proud.

One lesson on how to be a lady was to wear pantyhose or stockings, as she would call them. She taught me how everything should be nicely pressed when you place them in your closet or drawers. My mommita taught me the beauty of being a lady. She would often say, "*Mona, nobody wants a lady who doesn't take care of herself or her home! So don't go out of this house looking like a prima-donna while your room looks like a tornado hit it!*" To this day, I am still trying to figure out what a prima-donna is and what she looks like (lol), but all I knew growing up is that I didn't want to be an unclean one! My mother dressed me phenomenally. I had matching bows and matching ankle socks with ruffles. Not a detail was missed. I looked great, and she didn't spend a lot of money doing it either. She also sewed clothes. I remember her buying Simplicity and Butterick patterns, and I would hear her on her sewing machine, sewing masterpieces for me. The best outfit she made me was red pants that opened on the sides, revealing white on the inside. They were what we would call MC Hammer pants. My mother did that! I traveled from New York to Florida every summer to spend three months or so with my family, and they would always ask, where did you get your clothes from? I would proudly say, my mommy made them for me! Ahhh, precious memories, how they linger.

I watched my mom put on make-up, although, today, I am not a big fan. I watched her so meticulously apply products that enhanced her beauty. I remember the hot comb days. *LORD*, it was sheer TREACHERY!! TORTURE, I say! The things we did to beautify ourselves. Every Saturday before church in Brooklyn, NY, she would pull up one of our brown and yellow kitchen table chairs with a high back to the sink. She would turn it sideways, make me stand on it, and lean over the sink, holding on for dear life as I placed my head under the running water, which scalded me at first until she made the temperature just right. Then she would wash my hair. I prayed no soap got into my eyes because if it did, *HEAVEN* help me. The "burning eye" dance was no joke and often ended with bloodshot eyes.

We didn't have a blow dryer, so we had to let it "air dry," and it often did NOT dry all the way. She used the royal crown hair grease in the red cardboard can with the silver top and parted my hair in four squares. She would take the hot comb, fresh off of the fire, and head straight for the nape of my neck, to straighten the **"peas in the kitchen,"** as she would say. I would cringe and stiffen up until she made the first comb through, hearing the sound of sizzling hair grease as she moved down the hair shaft. At times, if there was too much grease, it would actually pop, and God help you if that hot grease, as small as those pops were, landed on your skin. I held my breath until I heard her put the comb back on the fire. Man, throughout the process, the smell of burning hair filled the air! I was burned on my neck, in the middle of my head, because that area was still wet and Lord save me when she got to my ears! I think I still have marks on the back of my ears because I would often get burned in the same place several times! However, when she finished, I felt like a princess! A burned one! But nonetheless, a beautiful princess!

We would go to the laundromat, and there I learned to wash, dry, and fold clothes. She took me to the grocery store, where I learned how to shop for a family. We would go to the Pathmark in Brooklyn, pulling a shopping buggy to carry our bagged groceries. I watched her squeeze the bread loaf to determine how fresh it was or read the labels on the milk and the orange juice to make sure they weren't expired. Mom taught me that when they want to get rid of something, they put it in the back, so make sure you move everything and pick the items from the back because they are fresh! I could still hear her, *"they think they're slick!"* We would then go to the meat market, where my mom would order various meats. She would order and say, *"can I have two pounds of bacon, thickly sliced,"* or *"give me two pounds of neckbones chopped small."* Then we would travel to the Chinese fish market, where she would order four red snappers, head off, and split! That's where I understood the fighting term. I will gut you like a fish! (lol) We would then stop by the vegetable stand, and I would learn how to touch and smell the right types of fruits and vegetables, not too ripe but just right.

    After a rough day, I remember mom had, she woke me up, did my hair, and we got dressed. She said let's go. My mom worked the night shift at Wyckoff Heights Hospital in New York, and she took public transportation late at night. I remember going to the bathroom, standing in the tub, and watching, waiting for her to walk up the sidewalk. I would see her, and it was like Christmas. I would wait to hear the key and run down the steps to give her a hug, my mom's hugs were like bear hugs. She was thin, but when she grabbed me, she held me so close, I could feel and hear her heartbeat, and she squeezed me, and I squeezed her. It felt like something we were waiting all day for and now that it is here, let's not rush but bask. After our embrace, I would follow her around, watch her settle in because all I wanted to do was be in her space, breathe the air she breathed, and walk in her steps. Take off her scrubs and her nursing shoes, and prepare water for her bath.

    She would be so tired, so she slept in late, and I would patiently watch everything from Sesame Street to Electric Company to Mister Roger's Neighborhood until she awakened. When she did, she cleaned the house from top to bottom and cooked dinner, only to get ready to go back to work, but this one particular day, she didn't go in. She decided to spend it with me. We jumped on the subway and traveled to Manhattan. I had never been to Manhattan. We dodged the crowds and the busy streets and arrived at a theater off Broadway. We saw "Momma, I Want To Sing!", and I believe that ignited my desire to sing. We laughed, we cried, and I was over the moon because I was with my mom.

We left the theater, and my mom took me to a restaurant where I ate my first steak. We laughed, and she talked, and I looked at my mom with eyes of admiration. The restaurant was dimly lit, and we sat in a booth. My first time in a restaurant booth, I believe that is probably why I love sitting in booths to this day. The booth was wood with black leather, nestled in a corner. It was an open kitchen, and I remember looking over the booth wall and seeing the chefs (I didn't know they were called chefs at the time) cooking. I was in awe and remember thinking, we are not in White Castles anymore! I sat across from my mom, and she taught me how to read the menu and how to order. We sat, and she would talk about her day, and then she would ask me, **"Mona, how was your day? Tell me all about it!"** That time with mom was so priceless. I remember it like it was yesterday. My mom would do anything to give me a moment of peace and happiness. She didn't have a lot of money at all, although she worked hard. I watched her roll pennies and save her change so she could buy extra things for herself. I watched my mom make something out of nothing, and I never knew anything different. She didn't belong to a particular church, but she went and took me with her. When I was introduced to the church, I jumped in headfirst, and my mom began to watch me. I remember her encouraging me to go to church. She was so proud of me. Because I came to church alone, I was adopted by so many people. I remember when my mom first heard me sing or, better yet, first heard me pray. I became her first prayer partner as she grew stronger and stronger.

I learned faith outside of the four walls of a church by watching my mother fall to her knees and pray. I learned how to love by watching the actions of my mother. I learned the meaning of home by watching how my mother cared for the home and created an environment where family meant something. Therefore, when I became involved in the Church, I learned how to read the written Bible and understood it at a young age because I watched the Bible come to life and become the living Word by the woman I was fortunate enough to call my mom. My walk with God led my mom to come to the physical church, and it whet her appetite for growing more in Him, but my mother was the church and didn't even know it!

She didn't go to church every Sunday, but she made sure I didn't miss a Sunday. She made sure I was there, and that was the start of my faith at a very young age. I would come home and share with my mom what I learned, and she would be so impressed. Even at my young age, my mom began relying upon me to help strengthen her faith by using the Word that was planted in me! I planted within her. It was watered. Then God gave the increase.

We grew together and endured hardships that caused me to grow up faster so I could be a support to her. By God's grace, I learned how to be her confidante. I learned how to care for the needs of my mother emotionally and spiritually while she cared for me physically. I learned to lean in when it was needed. To wipe her tears when they fell and how to get behind her and push her while she was pushing through. So when I say my mom was my best friend, it surpasses that, but there aren't any words that can fully capture what I feel. When her heartbeat, I felt it. When she is sick, I am sick with her. I rarely saw my mom angry, and when I did, it was because she allowed it to build up, and it reached its boiling point. I saw nothing but love for my mom, despite her trying to shield me from things. She was quiet and soft-spoken at times, and she hated to argue. I am grateful to have gotten that trait from her. When she laughed, she laughed with everything in her, and when she cried, it was equally the same. I was overprotective! If you looked at my mother wrong, I was all over you! She was the same for me! I remember when the whole school, well maybe not the whole school but at least 10, shoot, that felt like the whole school, wanted to fight me because I was the new kid. One girl who was the ringleader instigated it all! They had me hemmed up and pressed against the school fence, ready to fight until an adult stopped it. God had His Angels encamped around me that day! The next day, my mother got dressed, walked me to school, and said point them out, and when I tell you, she lit into them kids, and she did. Times were different back then, we had a village, and there weren't any ramifications for checking anyone if they were wrong. So when my mother laid it down, they picked it up, and I had no more worries! We were each other's protectors.

I remember when I was sick a few years ago, I didn't know what was wrong. My mom came to my house and took care of me like I was a small child. She bathed me, put on my clothes, fixed my food, then held me in her arms, rocking me as she cried out to God because I was in so much pain. I knew then that a Mother's love extends far beyond age. Once her baby, always her baby! It was things like that and countless others that time and space won't allow me to venture into that built and nurtured my relationship with my mom and made it so unique and strong that nothing could ever remove, replace or destroy....not even death.

Father God, In the Mighty and Precious Name of Jesus, I come before you as humbly as I know how to thank you for a Mother's Love! Thank you, my Heavenly Father, for giving us the gift of Mothers' Mothers who nurture, who love unconditionally and without end, who teaches by way of the life that they lead, who loves enough to discipline even when it hurts! Thank you, God, for the heart of every mother who may be reading this book right now! God continue to bless them, strengthen them and crown their heads with wisdom! Grant them the patience that they need, the guidance that they need and the discernment that will help them to cover their children fully. I pray for every relationship and every bond between a mother and a daughter, between a mother and son. That it will be strengthened no matter the age. If it is broken, God, I ask that you restore it! Draw them closer to each other, God, as they draw nigh to you. Then God, if there is someone who may not have the experience of a Mother's love, Lord, I ask you to raise up a woman who will be tailor-made and divinely placed to meet that need. God, thank you for being who you are, giving us what you have given. We thank you and praise you with all that we have and with all that we know! It is in Jesus' Precious Name that we pray and count it all done! Amen

Life Lesson:

"Do Something Good for Yourself!"

SELF-CARE

"Jesus said, "Come off by yourselves; let's take a break and get a little rest." For there was constant coming and going. They didn't even have time to eat."
Mark 6:31 (MSG)

For as long as I can remember, my mom was constantly on the go! She never stopped. She made you exhausted just watching her and guilty at the same time because you weren't doing anything. So as a child, I often hid (lol), so she wouldn't task me with things to do. As I got older, I learned how to piddle around when we were together so I wouldn't feel as guilty. Mom always worked the afternoon, three o'clock to eleven shift, so she got a chance to sleep in. However, when my mom came home after eleven, she took off one set of work clothes only to put on another set. She would not settle down until around one or two in the morning. It was incredible. As a CNA in a convalescent home, she cared for people all day! She lifted, tugged, cleaned, fed, you name it, she did it, and you would think that when she made it home, she would go straight to bed and not pass go or collect $200 (only Monopoly fans will get that one!), but she didn't. I remember being home one weekend. My mom had gotten cleaned up and was wide awake! She put a hamburger in the microwave to heat, prepared all of the fixings, and while doing so, we had a great conversation. She finished preparing her food, sat on the couch, and no sooner than five minutes, I heard this slight rumble. I glanced over, and there she was, fast asleep, hamburger bun in her hand, lettuce, tomato, burger, and all on the FLOOR! She was so tired but wired to keep going.

We, as women, have a tendency to do this all of the time. We go and go, always on the move! The term Superwoman, in one sense, can be viewed as a compliment because we have the strength to carry a lot and never miss a beat. However, the more I look at it, the more that I find that the term becomes a misnomer! Thereby causing a damaging mindset to ensue, resulting in women falling into a perpetual cycle of being constantly on the go and endeavoring to carry everything on our shoulders because we are "Superwomen!" Instilling an "if I don't do it, it will never get done!" mentality. Leading to more and more women neglecting themselves, losing sight of who they are, while continuously trying to pour from an empty cup that never seems to get refilled, striving to be everything for everybody, and by the time they look up, half of their life has passed by like a blurry memory.

I watched my mom feel guilty for sitting down, as though she would be reprimanded if she did. She had a routine. She would get up on Saturday mornings and clean the house. Back in the day, Aretha Franklin was the backdrop, and I could often hear her singing. In Brooklyn, we lived in an attached two-story home with a basement. We were so attached to the houses beside us that we could hear every move they made and vice versa. When Saturday came, they already knew, so we often found that they would make that their cleaning day as well. Our neighbors on one side of us were from Guyana and the other side from Brooklyn. We had a smorgasbord of cultures and nationalities on our block, and everyone knew everyone, and we looked out for each other. Across the street, we had a cleaners, and I would play with the owner's children growing up.

There was a storefront church that churched up a storm! I mean, they had a *good-good* church, tambourines, washboards, foot-stomping, hand-clapping all topped with off-key singing! They were from Haiti, so we did not understand what they were saying, but we knew they had something to praise God for! I remember my neighbor from Brooklyn going across the street one Sunday and telling the church they had to close their door because they were too loud! Now she had some nerves. I mean, I was young, but even I knew better than that! I stood far away so I wouldn't get struck by the lightning bolt that would be headed straight for her. Little did she know, my mom enjoyed every ounce of what she heard coming from that church. It made her feel good, it helped her to feel God…it helped her to remember who she belonged to!

Watching my mom and applying her lesson of doing something good for myself has ignited my passion for teaching and empowering women holistically! Encompasses teaching self-care, caring for your soul and yourself, and self-care, loving who you are unapologetically! I am addicted, in the best sense of the word, to helping women to understand their worth, helping them to know their worth and not accept any discounts. It is imperative that this mindset takes root within us, especially during the times that we are in. My mom didn't see Carolyn anymore. The Carolyn, who used to get up early on Saturday morning to clean the house! Mommy would turn on Aretha Franklin and sing to the top of her lungs. My mom could sing, and you better not speak to the contrary, even if she hit the wrong note! She would start moving her hands all around with each note, put her hand on her hip, that's when you knew the vocals just got real, and she would sing and sing until her housework was done! But somehow, somewhere, she lost who she was trying to be for others! Caring for others, doing for others, showing your support, and all that comes with that is good until it begins to overtake who you are. We have to have balance! Without balance, we are lost, and we inadvertently teach people, by way of our imbalance, how to treat us by the way we treat ourselves.

So soul-care, self-care, and self-love are paramount to our survival! We stand on the shoulders of the women within our ancestry, who raised ten to fifteen children with extremely limited resources, endured sicknesses with home remedies, built houses, and turned them into homes that were filled with love and compassion! We stand on the shoulders of women who educated their children while possessing limited education themselves! We tread the paths forged by beautiful women who exemplified strength beyond our wildest imagination! Now we don t-shirts that say "we are the dream of our ancestors", which is true, but we must understand that it far surpasses what we do for a living, but how we take care of ourselves, what we feed our minds, our body, and our spirit. It includes how we show love to ourselves and how we replenish all that we give out daily.

> Psalm 23:1-6
>
> *God, my shepherd! I don't need a thing! You have bedded me down in lush meadows. You find me quiet pools to drink from. True to your word, you let me catch my breath and send me in the right direction. Even when the way goes through Death Valley, I'm not afraid when you walk at my side. Your trusty shepherd's crook makes me feel secure. You serve me a six-course dinner right in front of my enemies. You revive my drooping head; my cup brims with blessing. Your beauty and love chase after me every day of my life. I'm back home in the house of God for the rest of my life.*

My mother's favorite scripture was Psalms 23. If you go into their home, you will find it amidst a load of scriptures she posted proudly all over the doors. She did this to constantly be reminded of what God's Word said about her. She fed her soul daily with His Word, which fed her soul! My mom practiced soul care daily! There are three parts to a man. Please note that it encompasses us as beautiful women when I say man. I probably didn't need to say that!

It is critical to understand how we are made up! We have to be cognizant of the many layers that exist within and the purposes of each component so that we can, ultimately, use all that we have to fulfill His plan! When we know how intricately God made us as creatures and how we are all uniquely tailored and designed, it helps us to embrace and love who we are fully. When we love ourselves, we will take the steps necessary to take care of our souls, which keeps us in tune with the Father, our Divine Potter, and the Creator of the beautiful Masterpiece, which is YOU! The human spirit is the deepest part of man. It is how we communicate with God in the spiritual realm! The Soul: who we are, our personality, it houses how we think, how we feel, how we respond! The Body: aka the vessel, the vehicle that allows us to connect and exist in the world! Our body houses the soul, and the soul is the vessel that contains the spirit. Three Parts That Makes Us One!: The Soul Tripartite!

> 1 Thessalonians 5:23-24
>
> "May God himself, the God who makes everything holy and whole, make you holy and whole, put you together—spirit, soul, and body—and keep you fit for the coming of our Master, Jesus Christ. The One who called you is completely dependable. If he said it, he'll do it!"

If you would indulge me for just a moment as I expound a little on how the Bible defines the Soul. In Genesis 2:7, it says that "God formed Man out of dirt from the ground and blew into his nostrils the breath of life. The Man became a living soul!" (MSG) He BLEW! If I take it a little further, the Greek: (New Testament Language) word and definition of "breath" is Psuche/Psyche to breathe! To blow! Therefore, our soul is the direct aftermath of God breathing His Gift of Life into a person! This means that God breathed into us His thoughts! His emotions! His Will! He made us in HIS image! Our Soul is the very breath of GOD!

Our soul is made up of three parts: the MIND of Man; The EMOTIONS of Man; The WILL of MAN! So let's break this down even further! The Mind, in two parts, conscious Mind-Where our thinking and reasoning is housed and subconscious: Where our deep belief and our attitudes are housed! **Psalm 23:7 (NASB)** *"For as he thinks within himself, so he is. He says to you, "Eat and drink!" But his heart is not with you."* What we think eventually starts to reflect who we are. Our thoughts become actions. Now I know we have heard this before! This scripture is an example of how we can think one way in our minds and feel a totally different way in our hearts! What we conceive in our minds, we manifest! The saying, whether we think we can, or we think we can't, we are right!

Another example is when you think in your mind that you are more than a conqueror, but in your heart, you feel defeated because of what you see! Moreover, you say, "I love me some me!" but you believe you are inadequate in your heart. You don't believe that you are worthy enough to take steps to take care of yourself!

My mom knew what she should do, but she didn't. It wasn't until my mom got older, I believe around 65 or a little later, that a light came on, and she totally shifted, and when I say shifted, my mom shifted! She started to do things that mattered to her regardless of what people thought. My mother got four TATTOOS! She got a new one every birthday, and they all represented something. She got two Angels because she loved angels! She got praying hands! She had her name tattooed on her! She had both arms and both legs tattooed, and I was not mad at her! She did something that I would have never thought she would do! She started speaking her mind and releasing things that did not matter. My mom had an "it is what it is" attitude. If I iron clothes today, good.

If I don't, oh well! If I cook tonight, great! If not, there are leftovers in the refrigerator, or better yet, you have two hands, cook for yourself. Mind you, it was just her and my dad in the home, so he was completely shook! He didn't know what to do! But He had to accept it! My mom began to rise up and take care of her! She awakened to the fact that if I don't take care of myself first, I will be no good to anyone else! If I don't nourish myself first with the Word, how can I build my home? Soul care arrived!

When we think of how our soul is made up of three parts, mind, emotions, and will. It is important that we understand those aspects as well. So when we focus on taking care of ourselves, we know what each component needs. Let's talk about our will first, shall we?

> Revelations 3:20 (NASB) "Look at me. I stand at the door, and I knock. If you hear me call and open the door, I'll come right in and sit down to supper with you.
>
> Deuteronomy 30:19 (The Msg) "I call Heaven and Earth to witness against you today: I place before you Life and Death, Blessing and Curse. Choose life so that you and your children will live." Jesus is a straight gentleman! He will never force Himself on any of us! He will never force us to believe anything that we do not want to believe. It has to be our choice! He lays it out plainly, so crystal clear, so we can make a well-informed decision! We have that choice! When WE make a choice to follow Him, it shows Him that we love him, that it is our desire to follow Him and to do His will! Even in the midst of our many failures, our ups and downs, and our distracted selves, He loves us and helps us to learn and get back on track!

We have the choice when it comes to our lives! We can choose to honor God with our lives! We can choose to feed our souls with the things that will help us make God-choices! The same holds true for taking care of ourselves, we have the choice, and the state of our mental, emotional, spiritual, and physical well-being is a direct result of that choice! Our emotions are defined as a conscious mental reaction (such as anger or fear) which is subjectively experienced as a strong feeling usually directed toward a specific object and typically accompanied by physiological and behavioral changes in the body. I find it just one of the vast, awesome things about Jesus that relates so much to us: everything that we experienced, He experienced and maintained who He was in all of his divinity! The emotions Jesus felt within the Bible are for us to see and relate to:

- Love: (Mark 10:21: Jesus looked at Him & loved him)
- Grief: (John 11:33-35: Jesus saw her weeping & He was moved)
- Joy: (Luke 10:21-Jesus full of joy with the Holy Spirit)
- Anger: (Mark 11: 12-17: cursed the fig tree/overturned tables)
- Frustration: (Mark 8:12- He sighed deeply in His Spirit)
- Sorrow: (Matthew 26: 37-38: my soul is overwhelmed with sorrow to the point of death)

Our emotions are triggered by so many various components of life that it is important how we manage them in an effort to take care of our souls. A key component to self-care! Our emotions, when allowed to overtake us, can make us do some things that we will either be lauded for or end up regretting! That spouse who caught their spouse in the midst of infidelity, back in the day, we would read about cars being keyed, windows being broken, all of that. Or, if we have a bad day, we resort to emotional eating, excessive retail therapy, or even unhealthy isolation. The key is to not fight our emotions but accept them and begin to work on the triggers that brought them on! In the Bible, we see so many accounts of Jesus expressing His emotions, but they never overtook Him! He calmly accepted where He was emotionally. He gave Himself time and space to let His emotions out! We must follow His example.

> *"Soul care is the daily process of cultivating healthy thought patterns and taking inventory of emotions so that you can walk in obedience and live freely before God while also healthily forming meaningful relationships with other people."* -JustDisciple.com

    I would watch my mom sit down and write out all of the household bills that were due for the month and try to make every penny stretch. When she found that something was going to have to be paid at another time, she would diligently get on the phone and make arrangements. My mom prided herself in making dollars stretch, but it weighed on her and had the tendency to cause undue stress trying to work it all out. Today, we face the many pressures of life with balancing home and a career. Working on climbing the proverbial ladder of success so as not to fall victim to the financial disparities that exist! Finding the strength to say NO and knowing that it is okay to remove the mask that so many of us wear to hide the truth of where we really are. Being free of these things is detrimental to proper soul care and self-care!

Psalms 46:5 (NIV): God is within her, she will not fall; God will help her at break of day.

Own where you are and stand in your truth! It's okay to not be okay! We do ourselves more harm than good by trying to wear the facade of always being okay. You are not being true to yourself, and if you aren't true to yourself, it will be impossible to be true to anyone else! Find someone who will allow you to be you without judgment! Someone who will let you take off the mask, show the "ugly" side of you, and help pray you through it without fear of them gossiping about you! Trust and believe this is vital! We have a lot of bone carriers in this world! If they take a bone, they will carry a bone, so you have to be prayerful and ask God to build your circle of trust!

My mom was that for me. We were that for each other. My mom would tell me things. I know she didn't tell anyone else, and as I got older and our relationship matured, she began to ask me to help her spiritually. We would talk about anything and everything! We kept each other's secrets! I would call my mom on a bad day and didn't have to say a word, and she would interpret my silence and just say, "Let it out, Baby-girl, I am here!" I miss that! We need that! We all need an outlet! When you find one, treasure it! Cherish it like a precious gem! They are hard to find! However, if you stop looking and start praying, God will move people and strategically place people who are in your corner around you, and it will be just what you need!

Realize that where you are is not your final destination! I heard my Pastor say, "don't put a period where God has placed a comma." Where you are is not final! We are always going! As a part of soul-care and self-care, learn to look at your situation and ask God what you are to learn from it. Ask what you can take from it and apply it so you can be better. Also, recognize that some of the things we go through are not for us but to help someone else! Some things also come not for us to react but to observe, take notes and wait for instruction! Learn to extend yourself some grace! If you didn't get it done, there is always tomorrow! We are so far from perfect, but we measure ourselves through a lens of perfection or by what we believe is perfection! Ask God to allow you to see yourself the way that HE sees you! An imperfect person striving to live by Grace and Mercy every day! Make taking care of YOU, physically, emotionally, and mentally a PRIORITY! You deserve it!

> *3 John 1:2 We're the best of friends, and I pray for good fortune in everything you do, and for your good health - that your everyday affairs prosper, as well as your soul!*

Soul-care and self-care are NOT SELFISH!

I mentioned earlier that my mom was an overthinker. She would think a lot and put herself in a space that wasn't always good or healthy. She would think of some of the things she went through and question why, and have thoughts on things that could never be changed. It thankfully never got out of hand, but we have to take care of ourselves mentally and normalize mental health. Everything starts in the mind. Every action, every step, starts within the mind. If we want to produce positivity, it starts with our thoughts because they eventually become what we do. We have to take steps to take care of ourselves mentally and not be ashamed. We have to have outlets that will provide us a place to unwrap and offload all that we have been carrying!

We have to be okay with being vulnerable so we can be healed. His strength is made perfect in our weakness! This means it is okay to not always be strong! Soul-Care and Self-Care are intertwined, and we cannot have one without the other! Just like in a workout, we cannot spot tone or lose weight in just one area. We have to work the entire body in order to get results! Soul care is taking care of your Mind! Your Emotions! Your Will! Self- Care is taking care of yourself spiritually, physically, and emotionally!

SOUL CARE CALL TO ACTION

How do you set time aside for just you and God?

_____

_____

How are you working on your relationship with Him daily?

_____

_____

What do you love most about your relationship with God?

_____

_____

What steps are you taking to take care of your soul?

_____

_____

How are you taking care of you? Write down what that looks like?

_____

_____

Name one thing that you will do to practice consistent Soul Care without compromise.

_____

_____

Take the necessary steps to take care of your soul! Set aside time where it's just you and Him.
Listen for His Voice, His Guidance, His Direction! Our soul is 100% worth it!

Life Lesson:

"Don't Take No Wooden Nickels" (Self-Love)

> *Or didn't you realize that your body is a sacred place, the place of the Holy Spirit? Don't you see that you can't live however you please, squandering what God paid such a high price for? The physical part of you is not some piece of property belonging to the spiritual part of you. God owns the whole works. So let people see God in and through your body.*
> 1 Corinthians 6: 19-20

"Don't take no wooden nickels, Mona!" As many times as I heard my mom make this statement, I never really understood what it meant at all. When I got older, I looked it up and found that it was an old American adage that advised one to be cautious of one's dealing. However, when I was younger, I learned the practical meaning of it! I used to go to the corner store in Brooklyn for my mom, and as a reward or a thank you, my mom would say, keep the change! So you know I was so excited and started picturing all the things in my head that I would buy with the change. The cashier would give me the change, and I went on my mission for treats! I went back to the same cashier that gave me the change to pay for all that I had, and he shook his head and told me he couldn't take the money. I was like, but you just gave it to me. Why? He replied, you have some Canadian coins in here, and they are no good in this store. I was so disappointed, but I learned that although it looked good, it showed signs of value at a glance. If I looked closer, I would see that they were really of no value at all. Hence, "don't take no wooden nickels, Mona," so much for all of the banana Now and Laters that I was going to buy.

I was always a different type of person. I didn't think the same as other kids my age. I believe it was because of the environment that I lived in and the fact that I saw so much within my immediate family that it caused me to grow up a little faster. I also spent a lot of time alone and within my thoughts, so I grew up with a need for validation in some areas, but I was always focused on excelling and figuring things out for myself and not relying upon people. This, I have found to be a plus, but it did pose a few challenges in the area of self-love.

By taking on the task of not relying upon others, I usually closed myself off for fear of rejection or not being able to fully express myself so others would understand. When I did open up, I often tried to please others more than myself, put myself on the back burner, and not take the much-needed time for myself. I often felt guilty if I said no, and little did I know, during those times that I was teaching people how to treat me, love me, care for me, and respond to me.

I watched my mother literally work her finger to the bone and did not get all of the appreciation that she deserved from others. She would spend her last on people and give until it hurts, but oftentimes it was not reciprocated. It wasn't until my mother reached her older stage in life did I see her start to break those chains that she wore and subconsciously placed on me. She started making her voice louder and saying no without hesitation, and it began to please her. She started re-introducing herself to those who thought they knew her well. When it came down to self-love, my mother did not fully embrace it. Now mind you, I never heard my mother talk down on herself or think she was less than who she was. She was a proud woman, in the good sense of the word, and walked with her head up high, but if you looked really close, you could see in her eyes that she felt she could be more, that there was more, but she didn't know how to move forward, so she settled.

I can recall looking at pictures of my mom in her earlier years, sporting her afro and short A-line dresses. She was beautiful, her smile was radiant, and she had an air of confidence that I pray would be replicated within my life. My mom would walk into a room, and her smile would light it up. She had a quiet nature but a loud and beautiful spirit that spoke stridently and caught attention when she walked into a room. She didn't say a lot and was extremely observant, but it was over when you got her started on a subject she loved to talk about! Getting back to her not embracing self-love, it was more in the physical, emotional, and spiritual aspects of life, and she made sure that she taught me to do the opposite of what she did. My mom was one who always looked for the other shoe to drop. She would often not allow herself to get happy about something or to get excited about things that may happen because she feared disappointment. So this caused her not to enjoy moments.

SELF LOVE TIP #1: ENJOY THE JOURNEY!

I will never forget someone shouted that to me, and it resonated so heavily within me. We are so worried about letting loose and dreaming. It may be because we have faced many disappointments that you find yourself saying, I cannot allow my heart to go through another one, but what I found is that we can attract the energy that we put out. Every journey that we are afforded to be on is meant to be enjoyed. God's plan for us is not to harm us but to give us an expected end! For I know the plans that I have for you! (Jeremiah 29:11) Our Creator, the One who called us and ordained us before time began, has a plan for us, and we just need to REST in that plan and follow His lead. We know that there will be much to learn, but also much to enjoy! There will be growing and stretching, which may not feel good all of the time, but if we trust Him, it will all work towards our expected end, as it is needful!

Don't look for things to go wrong! As my mother used to say, if you go looking, you may find just what you are looking for! Ask yourself, if I trust God, why am I afraid to turn the corner? If I believe that He is working all things together for my good, why am I waiting for the bottom to fall out? What is that saying to God? What does it say about our faith, or even more, what does it say about our trust, our belief in the promises of God? Did

HE not say it, and shall it not come to pass? (Isaiah 43:19). The best analogy I have is to use "courtship." The difference between courtship and dating is that with dating, you are reviewing your options, seeing what is out there, and moving with no intention or commitment.

Courtship, on the other hand, you know you are with the ONE! There is no need to seek the other, no need to keep on dating. You both agree that you are working towards the same end, and that is marriage. Since you know that, you can enjoy the journey of getting to know each other and all that it entails! You will savor those moments when you learn something new. You will enjoy the outings, the phone calls, and the quality time together because you know what you're working towards. On the converse, when there are disagreements, or the unintentional disappointments, the misunderstandings, and mishaps that are bound to happen, you don't throw it all away because the end is still the same. It's just all a part of the journey! So let go and allow yourself to enjoy the process of the journey. The end is the same, YOU WIN! So relax, relate, release! WOOSAH! Enjoy what you are privileged to have! Also, note that the story of your journey is designed to help someone else enjoy their journey!

ENJOY THE JOURNEY SELF CHECK

What journey are you currently on? *(There can be several but just list the most impactful one)*

_____

_____

What are you F.E.A.R.ful of? *(False Evidence Appearing Real?)*

_____

_____

How are you releasing the fear, so you can enjoy life? *(2 Timothy 1:7)*

_____

_____

How are you preparing to help others with your experience? *(Rev 12:11a)*

_____

_____

What are you believing in God for during, within, and at the end of your journey? *(Let's touch and agree)*

_____

_____

Instead of looking at what can go wrong, focus on what can go RIGHT because of Who is in Control!

> *Father God, your desire for us is to have life and to have that life more abundantly. God, you also desire for us to trust you in all things and know that you have a plan for us to prosper! Help us not to be stifled in fear but to walk boldly in all that you have called us to. I, now, God, touch and agree with all that is the changes that have been written, and I know that you will supply and give them the strength that they need to stand in who they are in YOU! It is in Jesus' Name we pray AMEN*

Self-love requires an inner self-check. A self-check from the neck up! You have to love who you are. You have to look inside yourself and spend time with yourself, and that may seem difficult at first, but when you truly want to love yourself, you will do what it takes to find out who you are. My mom knew who she was. She knew what she could take and what she would take and that intrigued me. She knew what she loved, she knew what would make her happy, and she knew how to enjoy being alone and enjoyed it, but the one tragic flaw my mom had was that she did not pursue it entirely. She stayed in situations that she knew she did not like until they became unbearable. Then she would yell and scream and say what she would do, and I, as a child and even in my adulthood, would encourage her, yes, Mom! Please go for it! Do you! I am here to support you! Only to watch the fire be extinguished and the flame fizzle.

When I was a child, the home circumstances were not the best, and my mother would always choose to do something different. She would change her sleeping arrangements, she would fight back, she would remain quiet and passive, and she would leave. She did many things to escape and grab hold of what she wanted, but something always drew her back in. Whether it was words that were spoken, the love for her home, and all that she helped to build, it was always something that caused her to return or to stay….to sit….in silence until it passed. Holding on to the hope that it was going to get better, that it was going to change, neglecting who she was. Neglecting the love she had for herself and sacrificing it for what she thought was going to be, and to this day, I believe my mom let go during her illness because once she knew I was okay, there was nothing left to hold on to. She didn't want to come back to the same struggle, the same uncertainty. I believe my mother saw a glimpse of what she always wanted and decided to finally pursue it even if it meant leaving this life and leaving me.

SELF LOVE TIP #2:
KNOW WHEN TO SAY WHEN AND KNOW WHEN TO WALK AWAY!

Please know when to say WHEN! Love yourself enough to WALK away from toxic things, toxic environments, and toxic people who wear the cloak of love, but it is nothing close to love. They can be family, your partner, a friend, or a foe! Pain and hurt usually come from the one closest to you! As it is unexpected! Toxicity is hazardous to your health. It eats away at your self-esteem, your self-confidence, and your self-love and disguises itself in phrases like, *"that it's me?"* *" Is it my fault?"* *You begin to ask, "what have I done?", "what did I do to deserve this?" "Why did this happen?" "I am not good enough?" I don't deserve anything better?" "God is punishing me for my past?"*

These false statements translate into guilt and unnecessary ownership of another's feelings and issues, thereby causing you to stay in situations that you should have left a long time ago. This can be the foundation of anxiety, depression, nervous breakdowns, and feelings of unworthiness that can distract you and cause you to stray away from the very destiny that God has designed for you to fulfill. **SAY WHEN AND WALK AWAY!** Love, self-love, does not hurt! Your peace is way too expensive to spend on things, people, and circumstances that are not worth the paper that money is printed on! They dump on you then they go on with their day, leaving you to carry a load that you were not assigned! Understand the assignment! The assignment is to love yourself! Replenish and refill your cup!

They always use the analogy of when you are on a plane, if it starts to have issues, before you try to put the oxygen mask on someone else, put it on yourself FIRST! You cannot help others to breathe if you are gasping for air! Self-love is not selfish! I will say that again for the folks in the back of the room, **SELF LOVE IS NOT SELFISH**! You want to present the very best of yourself to the world and not give out sloppy leftovers that you wouldn't even accept for yourself.

You are fearfully and wonderfully made (Psalm 139:14). What you have within you was made just for you and no one else! What the world needs from you, no one else can offer! The lane that you are driving in, others can attempt to drive in it, but they ultimately will not succeed! So how do you do this? You have to go back to what I said in the beginning, know yourself, so you can love who are unapologetically! Love yourself enough so that you can live out loud and proud! Love every part of what makes you, YOU! Do not leave your happiness, your feeling of self-worth, in the hands of anyone else! It is your responsibility!

KNOW WHEN TO SAY WHEN AND WHEN TO WALK AWAY SELF CHECK

How much do you love yourself on a scale of 1 to 10? *(1 being I need to do better - 10 being no one can love me better)*

_____

_____

How do you CONSISTENTLY show yourself, love?

_____

_____

How comfortable are you with saying "NO?" Do you have a sense of guilt?

_____

_____

What IMMEDIATELY needs to change so that the love that you have for yourself GROWS?

_____

_____

How will you set these expectations with your family and friends, so they support you?

_____

_____

Let go of the "Superwoman" concept so you can stop trying to save the world while loving yourself!

> *God help us to recognize that you did not call us to take on more than you have assigned for us to take on. Father, help us to love ourselves enough to know when to say when. Give us the desire to take care of ourselves so that we are fit and ready to follow the plan you have called us to. God, you told us in Your Word that we cannot pour new wine into old bottles, or they will break. Help us to learn to replenish ourselves. Teach us to take care of ourselves physically and mentally without guilt or hesitation. God, we rebuke the Superwoman complex and bind it up in the name of Jesus! We ask that you release time for peace and restoration daily, God. Help us to love ourselves and how to teach others how to treat us by the way we treat ourselves! All these things we ask in your Mighty and Matchless Name, AMEN!*

God, our Creator, looks at each of us as His Masterpiece. Inside and out, He made us into who He desired us to be!

> *Jeremiah 18:6 (The Message) "Can't I do just as this Potter does, people of Israel?" God's Decree! "Watch this Potter. In the same way that this Potter works his clay, I work on you, people of Israel.*

We are the ones that bring about the unsureness and issue with who and what we are. In all aspects, from physical to spiritual. We hit God with a barrage of questions rooted in insecurity. The media plays a part. What we see, whether we want it to or not, shapes and forms our perception of what beauty, skill, and talent are, just to name a few. They display a skewed perception that is so far from what God, the Master Potter, considers a masterpiece! We, again, are His creation, His masterpiece, and in God's Eyes, we are beautiful just the way we are.

We also take on a persona that doesn't reflect our God nature, that doesn't reflect the Image, His Image that we were created from. We start taking on jealousy and envy. We start converting the gifts and talents of others and neglect our own. The Bible states that everything was created for a purpose, and we cannot have one without the other.

> *1 Corinthians 12: 21-26 "The eye cannot say to the hand, 'I don't need you!' And the head cannot say to the feet, 'I don't need you!' so that there should be no division in the body, but that its parts should have equal concern for each other. If one part suffers, every part suffers with it; if one part is honored, every part rejoices with it."*

So changing who we are is not part of the original design. God can work and use us no matter what. But if HE created us to be "just right," why do we often seek to change? My mother would always comment on my legs. She would say *you have big, thick, beautiful legs!* She would say *you get them from your father's side because all of our legs look like pencils, like bird legs.* She said *they are like number one legs. They go straight up and down!* We would laugh, but in the back of my mind, I did not want my legs. I wanted hers! How ironic! I thought my legs were "cankles," you know, "cankles", that's when your calf and your ankles run together. There was no line of separation! My mom called her pencils, and I called mine magic markers. So when I acquired a trainer, shaping my calf muscles was high on the list. However, no matter what I did or how much weight I used during my calf raises, my legs still did what they wanted to do. Until one day, I looked at my legs in boots and heels, and I was like….. "Wait a minute, they look nice! I love my legs," and the rest is history!

That was the physical component, but there was also the spiritual component. I knew God called me, and my mother knew as well. She would often tell me that she was not going to be satisfied until she saw me speaking and singing from the pulpit. She was hard set on this, and I wasn't! I compared myself to other people and would talk myself out of things because I wasn't able to expound as fiercely as the others, or I was not able to perform all of the vocal acrobatics that other singers did. But my mom sat me down and reminded me of who I was in God or rather who she saw me be in Him. My mother always called me to expound on the scriptures for her. When she had a question or didn't understand something from the Sunday sermon, she would call me. I would talk, cross-referencing other scriptures, applying it to practical life so she could understand and she would say *see, that is* what I am talking about! Others need to hear all of this, all of what God has placed in you!

My mom called me one day and said, "Mona, I want to increase my faith. I want to read more. Can you show me how?" I gave her a starting point and then sent her the Bible verses we were reading on a daily basis at my church, and I watched my Mother start to flourish spiritually. My mom would often stop and tell me if you could only see what I see in you or, better yet, what God sees in you!

SELF LOVE TIP #3: PRAY AND ASK GOD TO LET YOU SEE YOU THE WAY HE SEES YOU!

If you are here reading this book, please know and embrace the fact that you were created with and for a purpose! You were tailor-made to fulfill God's purpose during your lifetime. You just have to seek to find out what it is and then move with purpose. Some people are blessed to know from day one what their purpose in life is. They know what they are gifted with. They know exactly what to do to get it accomplished. Some of us are not that fortunate! Some find out in their older years what they are called to do, and trust me, that is okay because God's timing is perfect, and whenever you find out, it is exactly when you were supposed to! So don't let when you know affect how you move!

If we could only see ourselves the way that God sees us, it would help us in every aspect of our lives. When we connect to the purpose for which we were created, we would see that everything that lives within us is just what we need to navigate through this life while pleasing God. We have to trust that God knows what He is doing and not question Him. We have to know that every aspect of our life is planned, and He walked it out! We have to stand firm in the knowledge that God does not make mistakes and all things really do work together for our good.

I know, easier said than done! What I found is sometimes we don't ask because we may not like the answer we may receive. Why? We may have it all figured out in our head what we want to do, what we believe we are called to, what we feel we are gifted with, and God may say, "pump your brakes! That's not it!" His plan may actually take us into the unknown. It may stretch us beyond our comfort level. It may cause us to search deeper within ourselves to notice things we may not have wanted to notice! It may cause us to deepen our prayer life and our study time. It may cause us to cut ties and sever relationships that do not line up with our purpose so we can be in alignment with what His plans are for us! It just may cause anxiety because we have to relinquish control and really exercise faith and walk the walk we talk about and proclaim that we are already walking! AHHHHHHH! Scary, I know! Get the picture?

Do not be afraid to define your dash! The dash between the day you were born and the time you transition back home to the Creator. Define your dash! What impact did you make because you carried out what God had set for you to do! Did you make the world better because you were there! Did you impact lives! Did you help point someone to Him? Did your testimony inspire and encourage someone to keep going! Are you pleased with the life you led? If you asked God, and He allowed you to see you the way He sees you, then you will be able to answer these queries in the affirmative when that time comes. Or did you live life like the man who buried the one talent that God gave Him instead of working to give God a return on the investment that he made in him!

Matthew 25:14-21 NKJV - "For the kingdom of heaven is like a man traveling to a far country, who called his own servants and delivered his goods to them. And to one he gave five talents, to another two, and to another one, to each according to his own ability; and immediately he went on a journey. Then he who had received the five talents went and traded with them and made another five talents. And likewise, he who had received two gained two more also. But he who had received one went and dug in the ground and hid his lord's money. After a long time, the lord of those servants came and settled accounts with them. "So he who had received five talents came and brought five other talents, saying, 'Lord, you delivered to me five talents; look, I have gained five more talents besides them.' His lord said to him, 'Well done, good and faithful servant; you were faithful over a few things. I will make you ruler over many things. Enter into the joy of your lord.'

Give God back a double and triple-fold return on the investment, He so graciously made. He in you! Get excited about it! Get excited about knowing that God, who is Omnipotent and Omniscient, made a plan just for you, and it is better than any we could ever conjure up for ourselves! You are a beautiful Masterpiece, the Eye of the Father, so fall in love with the plan God has designed just for you!

PRAY AND ASK GOD TO LET YOU SEE YOU THE WAY HE SEES YOU SELF CHECK

When you look in the mirror, what do you see?

_____

_____

How would you describe your *Spiritual* self confidence?

_____

_____

Do you think that you see yourself the way God sees you?

_____

_____

Do you know your purpose? What has God shown you about yourself?

_____

_____

What gifts do you possess? Are you using them?

_____

_____

You are called for purpose! No one exists just to exist! Ask God to show you His purpose for you! Ask Him to allow you to see YOU the way He sees you! When He does, walk boldly in what you see! Those ordained to be touched by you are waiting!

> Father God, please bring Psalm 139:14 to life within us! Help us to be deeply rooted in Your word that states that we are fearfully and wonderfully made! We are your Masterpiece, a Designer's original! Everything we are and everything that we can hope to be lies within you! Help us to tap into the gifts and the beauty that you have placed inside of each of us. Help the person who is holding this book today and praying this prayer to know they are loved, they are beautiful, they were created with and for purpose! Open our eyes, God, to see us the way that YOU see us, God! If there are any reading today that may not know their purpose, God, I intercede on their behalf and ask you to reveal it to them, God, so they can walk within the path that you have ordained specifically for them! We thank you, God, for creating us in your Image and with Your Purpose! In Jesus' Name, we pray, AMEN

My mom and I would talk about relationships and what we wanted. She would tell me stories about the suitors she had in her younger days and what it meant for her. She said *she didn't have many, and the ones that she was interested in were not interested in her.* She shared stories of how she felt like a second choice, a backup plan. She expressed to me how she didn't know love or even felt it, and that broke my heart. Although she was okay, I could hear how that impacted her. I hate to fathom that my mom left this earth without feeling the true love of a man and woman, from her point of view, the way that God intended.

My mom and I never had the "birds and the bees" conversation. When I reached the milestone of "womanhood" by my body's standard, she just explained what was happening and said, "Okay, Mona! NO boys!" It is funny to think that during that time, that's all it took to stay on the straight and narrow. Two words, "No Boys," and I took heed to those words. I didn't ask any clarifying questions, my curiosity wasn't peaked, and no feelings of rebellion rose up within me. She said no, and my attitude was, enough said! I wish we could go back to those days, as I look at the plight of the world today, but that, in and of itself, is another topic, for another day and another book!

Little did my mom know, I was reliving her pattern of love. I had some relationships, not very many, but they did not lead to anything. Then I got married, which my mom emphatically said, *was not sanctioned*. It ended in divorce. I have been unattached ever since. My mother always prayed for that aspect of my life to be filled with someone who would love me and show me what she didn't have. So when it was time to fantasize, we did it together. My mother also prayed that I would embrace this time of "singleness" and enjoy it. Enjoy it because I don't want to lock myself into something with someone, label it a marriage and produce fruits of unhappiness! So she said wait, it will all be worth it! I followed my Mother's orders and began to pray that God would work on me, take away the things that would hinder me from experiencing love the way that He intended, and make me ready. While He was and still is working, I am serving, listening, and applying! Not manipulating, searching, plotting, or scoping as that leads to failure! I spoke about courtship earlier, or rather gave an analogy, and I would like to add more context to that at this juncture. I desire courtship and the aspect of courtship, the learning, the growing, the preparing while knowing what the expected end will be. As a result, I am learning to allow God to be God in my life and His revelations are mind-blowing, bringing to life this scripture:

> Philippians 4:19 - *You can be sure that God will take care of everything you need, his generosity exceeding even yours in the glory that pours from Jesus.*

SELF LOVE TIP #4: ALLOW GOD TO BE GOD IN YOUR LIFE!

Please move in real close. I have a secret to share. Did you know that God will show you how you are to be treated, by the way, He treats you (mic drop)? When you allow God to be God in your life, He will show you who He is to you and for you! When my mother passed, I felt like my covering on this Earth was gone. Who is going to pray for me, be there to comfort me, talk to me when I need encouragement, who will be there to answer my questions, and give me guidance and direction? I felt lost, naked, uncovered.......alone. When God said in His Word that *He will never leave you nor forsake you,* He meant it. (Hebrews 13:5) God is concerned about you and everything concerning you!

I remember vividly crying out to God, asking Him to take care of me in ways that I never knew I needed. I needed Him to heal my heart, to ease the hurt and the pain. I needed Him to be for me what I knew no one else could be! I needed Him to show me who He is! When I tell you God is doing that, I tell no lies. God speaks in everything, and He guides us in all things if we just listen. If we are quiet long enough to hear that small voice that speaks so eloquently within us. If we stop ignoring the urges and the unction, those urges, those things that are pressing upon our spirits to do or to stay away from that, we feel and recognize that those just may be signs that God is trying to tell us something.

There are so many examples I can give! I was leaving the gym, and God told me to walk around my car. I was like, really, God? It kept pressing and pressing, and when I finally gave in, there was a huge nail pressed in my tire. Not enough to puncture and cause damage, but if I had backed up on that nail, I would be spending hundreds on a new tire. Another example, I went to a huge football game. I parked my car and looked back and thought I saw the lights on. I brushed it off and told myself that they would go off. I carried on and made a few stops. Mind you, there were 55k people at this game. A petition worker asked me to fill out a petition, I normally do not do it, but I did. Right at that moment, a lady whom I had never seen before stopped me and told me my lights were still on in my car! What is the likelihood that this lady would be at the same place where I was at that moment to let me know my car lights were on? I walked back and found my car still RUNNING. I cannot tell you the MAGNITUDE of

God's protection in all things! He cares about you enough to put you in place to receive things that you were not even expecting! God will take care of every DETAIL concerning your life! If we TRUST Him. I find myself saying that I feel sorry for the man that comes into my life because after seeing how I am supposed to be treated and how things are supposed to be taken care of when it comes to me, by God, Himself, then that man would have shoes He would never be able to fill! Then God taught me and changed it even as I typed these lines. If He is the Man I sent, he may not be able to fill my shoes, but He will know how to bend His knees to ask me to supply him with what He needs concerning you, and that is all you need! Trust me with the details! Trust me with your heart! Trust me, and allow me to be who I am! Allow me to be God in your life!

LET GOD BE GOD IN YOUR LIFE SELF CHECK

What do you love the most about your relationship with God?

_____

_____

Can you honestly say that you trust Him with every aspect of your life?

_____

_____

If you answered No, to the question above, what are you holding onto and why?

_____

_____

I challenge you to write down things that you need to relinquish control over, so you can be released to accept His love! Write those things down, and let's pray together!

_____

_____

God can love you in ways that no one else can! Don't miss out on that love, that love that comes without condition! Open your heart and mind so you can fully receive!

> *Lord, the most important relationship we will ever have is our relationship with you. It is in that relationship that everything is hinged upon. Help us to focus on deepening our relationship with you by reading your Word, fasting, and praying. Helps us, Lord, to make you our number one priority, and everything else will follow. God, remove those things that take your place within our lives! Move those things out of the way that hinders the growth of our relationship. God helps us to love the things that you love and to hate the things that you hate so we can be more like you! We were created to give you worship and praise, God;*

help us to do what we were created to do! Help us to realize that the only thing that matters is living a life that is pleasing to you! In Jesus' Name, we count it done! AMEN

Growing up, my mom wouldn't let me go just anywhere, and she did not let me bring just anybody home! She always prefaced it with, "Mona, everybody is not your friend!" "You cannot eat at everybody's house!" and the infamous, "I don't care what they do at their house, THIS is my house!" I asked to stay the night at a friend's house, who just lived down the block, and my mother said no! She didn't even blink her eyes when she said it. It was like she said No, and now what? My mother was not to be played with! She said what she said! Me, wanting to go, pleaded my case anyway because she knew this friend, she knew where they lived, she knew their parents, and she still said no BECAUSE she knew where they lived and knew their parents! Ha! Didn't make sense until I got older! Never doubt a mother's intuition! They know! To this day, my mother told me who my friends were and also told me who to leave alone. Some advice I heeded and some advice I didn't......I wish I had taken heed to all of it, but I learned very valuable life lessons through those teachable moments!

My mother felt like she didn't have any close girlfriends, she had one whom they connected with from time to time, but she didn't have friends who she felt understood her and allowed her to be who she was without apology. That is another reason why we were so close. We were best friends, we talked about any and everything, and we looked to each other for support. We were mother and daughter, but she trusted me as her friend when I grew older and could understand. She saw me as someone who would pray for her, comfort her, give to her when I could, be there when she needed to cry, hold her hand, help her with decisions, just be there to fill a space that she needed to have filled. That is why we were so closely knit, and I was extremely overprotective of her feelings and how she was treated. We had each other's back without hesitation or compromise.

I have learned to ask myself, why are people connected to me? That is so important! You have to re-evaluate your friendships and view your friendships the way God would have you to view them! Use the word of God as a filter.

> *Proverbs 27:17 - You use steel to sharpen steel, and one friend sharpens another.*

You should be growing from the people who are within your circle, and you should be helping the same people grow. If you find someone who is only there for what they can get or to "leech" upon what you have and who you may know in an effort to benefit themselves, run fast and run far! You should feel like you are valued and that you add value to every connection that you make. Ask yourself a major question, are the people that you are aligning yourself with also aligned with your purpose! You have to be careful with who you align yourself with because not everyone is equipped to handle where you are going, and because they are not, they may weigh you down! They may distract you from moving towards your purpose! They may try to sabotage or thwart your progress because what you are doing is not about them, and they cannot have what you have! EVERYONE THAT IS PATTING YOU ON THE BACK IS NOT PATTING WITH AN EMPTY HAND! I will sit that right there and pray you get that before the end of this book.

SELF LOVE TIP #5: BUILD YOUR FAITH SQUAD!

Your alignment matters! Love yourself enough to check who you are calling a friend! It is okay to have a small crew, a small squad, as long as it is a real squad! It is not about quantity but all about quality! People think I am joking when I say my circle is so small. It resembles a period! I could be no more serious when I say that! I don't need my phone ringing off the hook. I don't need the large crowds! Nor do I desire invites to be at every event going on or to hang with every Tom, Dan, or Jane! I just want friends who are real, trustworthy, loyal, and true, and in return, I give back the same realness, the same trustworthiness, and loyalty, and I am good! I need those friends who will allow me to be me unapologetically! I can be who I am without judgment, and they can be who they are in the same manner!

Folks who I can call my Faith Squad! Those who are not just in my circle but who are also in my corner! There is a difference! They believe in whom I believe in! They trust His report! They seek Him for guidance and answers before giving me advice! They will go to the War room in prayer for me! They are not afraid to shut me down when I am wrong, lift me up when I am to be celebrated! They help push me towards my purpose, and I, in turn, help push them! No jealousy, no envy, no strife. Will the friendship be perfect? NO! But will it be worth it! ABSOLUTELY!! I don't strive to be well known, but I strive to be worth knowing, and my circle should reflect the same!

BUILD YOUR FAITH SQUAD SELF CHECK

What does your circle of friends look like?

_____

_____

Are you able to be who you are without apology? Can they freely correct you if needed?

_____

_____

Would your circle of friends remain the same if you asked God to build your circle of friends?

_____

_____

Are the ones in your circle also in your corner?

_____

_____

Do you receive as much as you give? Is there a friendship balance?

_____

_____

Do a friend check! It matters who you are around! It matters who feeds into you! Don't for a moment think that your friends don't matter because they do!

> God, we come before you, asking you to build our circle of friends! Those that add to our lives and help us to add to theirs! We ask God that you remove those people who are not a part of our purpose from our lives, those who drain, those who attach to us for the wrong reasons, and those who do not have our best interest at heart! God surround us with true friends that love you, and that will love us with that same love. Help us to sharpen their iron as they sharpen ours. God, please give us the gift of discernment to know and recognize the motives of those around us and the boldness to walk away from those who are not right for us. God help us to take ourselves out of the way, so we will be open and receive who you have destined to be in our lives. Help us to understand God that they may not look like who we think they should, but help us to know they will be aligned and attached to our purpose, and that is all that matters! Help us to leave every door that you close, God, CLOSED! We thank you for not just those that

are in our circle but for those that are in our corner! For there is a difference! Thank you, God, for giving us true friends! In Jesus' Name, AMEN

A Test of Faith

"No test or temptation that comes your way is beyond the course of what others have had to face. All you need to remember is that God will never let you down; he'll never let you be pushed past your limit; he'll always be there to help you come through it."
1 Corinthians 10:13

Isaiah 38:26 *"Hezekiah turned away from Isaiah and, facing the wall, prayed to God: 'God, please, I beg you: Remember how I've lived my life. I've lived faithfully in your presence, lived out of a heart that was totally yours. You've seen how I've lived, the good that I have done.' And Hezekiah wept as he prayed—painful tears. Then God told Isaiah, 'Go and speak with Hezekiah. Give him this message from me, God, the God of your ancestor David: 'I've heard your prayer. I have seen your tears. Here's what I'll do: I'll add fifteen years to your life. And I'll save both you and this city from the king of Assyria. I have my hand on this city."*

When I think about crazy faith, in my terms of belief, it is truly believing that something can and will happen despite the fact that every single solitary thing looks like this isn't happening! I had no clue how devastating my mother's cancer was, no clue. The doctors never gave a stage that it was in, they did not specify what type, and they never used the word metastasized. It seemed the more questions we asked, the more medical teams that waltzed in and out of the room, and the muddier it was. I researched so I could ask questions, I asked them to speak in layman's terms, I yelled, I hollered, I apologized, I did all that I could until one day, I told them to imagine that the one person that they loved more than anything was lying in this bed, what would you want the doctors to tell you and how?

They had my mom go through radiation that did not do anything at all. They gave my mom such strong doses of medication that she would be out for hours, and when she did wake up, she woke up in pain, disoriented and non-communicative. But no matter what I saw, no matter what, I still believed. I had to start telling the doctors to stop talking around my mom because she could still hear and be careful with what you spoke around her. Stop speaking of death when my mom clearly said she wants to live. Stop treating her like she was gone when she was still here. My mom did everything she could to show them she wanted to live. Every test they put her through, she worked hard to pass. When they asked her questions, after tons of medication, she answered what she could, and they deemed that as she was not improving until I got so fed up and asked how do you expect her to remember when she is heavily medicated. I remember the doctor coming in and asking her where she worked and what the number was. She was able to tell them exactly where she worked. However, she got the number wrong. When the doctor left, she said, I knew that. I am so sorry, I won't do that again, and I broke down on the inside.

The same doctor wanted me to make the decision on the spot to put my mom in hospice, and at that time, I didn't want to think about hospice. He pulled me outside, looked me in the eye, and said, do you know how serious this is? There is nothing more we can do. Your mom is at the end-of-life stage. I could have literally screamed. I walked back into the room, numb, speechless, and in utter disbelief. I looked at my mom, my shero, my earth angel, and I declared I was going to pray for her out of this! I was going to have faith and believe! I was not going to accept what was being said! I knew who I believed in! I refused to talk to anyone about my mom being terminal, and I refused to let them say it to me, to my mom, or anywhere near her! I told my family if they could not speak positively or believe the same way that I did, then please do not come around.

I told the nurses, again, not to do their staffing change reports in my mother's room because all she would hear was the end-of-life statement, and that was not good at all. They didn't think so, but I knew. It was proven when my mom came home for a brief while, and she started talking to us, and she asked, "How would you all feel if all you heard all day was that you were going to die?" That shocked us all, but I told them. **A side note: Please watch what people speak over your loved ones when they are in the hospital or under a doctor's care. It matters.** Due to COVID, I couldn't stay overnight with my mom, so I did my best to control what I could while I was there.

The doctors told us that the cancer was everywhere except her brain. I took that, and I stood on that as proof that this was going to turn around. I would travel from Gainesville to Orlando three days out of the week, and I would pray, with every trip, that I would walk in, and my mom would be sitting up, talking. I took pictures of my mom when she was in her early debilitating state so I could show her before and after. I checked her daily medical briefs to see her weight gain and check for improvements. I had what others coined crazy faith. I just couldn't give up. I literally would cry, yell and scream when I prayed. I prayed until I had no voice left! The scripture regarding Hezekiah was the one I stood on. My mom couldn't turn her face to the wall for herself, so I did. I told people who told me that I needed to face reality, that if the roles were reversed and it was me lying in that bed, my mom would never give up believing. She would pray until she couldn't pray anymore! She would tear down the walls of her prayer closet until I came through, so I am going to do the same for her.

However, the more I prayed, the worse her condition became. She totally stopped communicating, stopped opening her eyes, and the life she had in her began to fade. She was swelling to the point where if you touched her skin, your fingerprints would remain…. Even still, I saw all of this but still believed. When I took my mom to a doctor's appointment at an earlier point in time, we sat in the waiting room, and she started talking to me. She said, "you know that song? You Made a Way?" I told her yes! She said you know, the part where the songwriter says they were planning his mother's funeral and God healed her, I replied yes again. She said with a strong voice of confidence, that is going to be me! You watch and see! That is going to be me, so don't cry! Be strong! So every time I went into the room, I reminded her about what she said! I played the song in her ear! Hoping that it would whisper just what she needed to stay with me....but God had other plans.

> "Faith is being sure of what we hope for and certain of what we do not see" (Hebrews 11:1).

No one else saw what I saw. I was working to look past what I saw physically and began to see my mom spiritually as I wanted her to be. I tried to see past the tubes, the fractured hip. I tried to see past the tremors, the disorientation. I tried not to hear her speaking to family and friends who had passed on. I tried so hard to not see the obvious. Faith is having a belief in something or someone. It is the most important element that we, as Christians, as children of God, possess. We believe in a God that we have not seen in the physical, that we have not seen with the natural eye, but we know by evidence of His Word and how He shows up in our lives that He exists and lives inside of those who choose to believe! We have faith, the word of Vanessa Bell-Armstrong that sees the invisible, expects the incredible and receives the impossible! I have Faith that I can conquer anything! Faith that uproots our problems, Faith to know that God can solve them.....Faith that can conquer anything! That faith that can only come by hearing the true, unadulterated Word of God, by the one whom He has sent! Faith that we must possess, or it will be impossible to please God! **(Hebrews 11:6)**

Allow me to dive deeper and share my studies with you! Faith in Hebrew is **Emunah.** This means firmness, steadfastness, fidelity **Emunah** appears forty-eight other times in the Old Testament, mostly as faithfulness or faithfully. In Greek, the root word from which we get faith, the noun is **Pistis**, and 'believe,' the verb is **Pisteuo**. **Pistis**, which means belief, trust, confidence, and fidelity. **Pitis** appears over 200 times in the New Testament. **Pistis** comes from the root word **peitho**, which means to persuade, have confidence, and come to trust. In summation, faith believes with absolute and complete confidence that God can and that He will! It is believing when you cannot see! Trusting Him when you cannot find Him! Knowing that God will keep His promises! That everything that is written from Genesis to Revelations is true! Faith is knowing that you know, that you know because He has proven Himself over and over to you and shown you who He is! HE has never failed us no matter how many times we have failed Him! God is God all by Himself and is able. Our Faith, again, is a firm, steadfast confidence in God. It is steady, unwavering, and lasts forever!

Our faith is tested daily and makes us stronger:

> *James 1:2-4 - Consider it all joy, my brethren, when you encounter various trials, knowing that the testing of your faith produces endurance. And let endurance have its perfect result so that you may be perfect and complete, lacking in nothing.*

If we saw everything and knew exactly what was going to happen in the day, traveling through life would be easy. If we were given the heads up on every trial and tribulation that we were going to encounter or every disappointment that was going to enter our lives, we would start to do what they call preventive maintenance, we would prepare and brace ourselves to not only receive the blow, but we may even go as far as to try to avoid it altogether. Where is the faith in that?

If God told us everything, He had in store for us, how would we develop our faith. How will we ever know how capable God is! How would we learn to trust Him or stand on His Word? A child that goes through school is given so many lessons that help them to grow and expand their knowledge on whatever topic they are learning. Each lesson is designed to build upon another and provide insight that we never knew existed. The best teachers are able to present information in such a way that children are clamoring to learn more, their interest is ignited, and they want to learn more. When they are excited about what they learn, and they are stretched, they retain more, they can recall information, and they can put it all together and make the necessary connection to prove that the lesson has accomplished its mission.

At the end of every lesson, there is a test. A test of your knowledge and if you paid attention and the student took plenty of notes, they will pass the test with flying colors. On the contrary, if you don't study, there will be nothing on the inside to bring back to your remembrance, or even worse, if someone gives you the answer, the gem of gaining knowledge is lost because you haven't experienced all that came with learning the lesson. With each test that you pass, you go to a higher level! Your mindset expands. You know how to study! You know how to go back to previous lessons, so you can see what has been done and move with that same tenacity even more because you have done it before! The more you learn, the more you know. The more you study, the more you retain! The more you retain, the stronger your knowledge base becomes! The more you know, the more you can share! The more you share, the more people are helped! The cycle goes on and on.

So it is with faith! The more life lessons we go through, the more we learn about God because He shows up differently in each lesson. When there is something within us that God needs to strengthen, a test will come, and we will stay in that lesson until we pass the test. God teaches us through each lesson how to study, how to seek Him within the scriptures, and how to apply the scriptures to our situation to help us to get stronger. When we walk through the lesson and not abort the process, our faith in God grows. We start approaching our challenges with the expectation of gaining knowledge. We get stronger because we have been through something! Our faith has been tested when we pass the test. God just doesn't take us through things for the sake of taking us through. It is to develop us as Christians. To help us to get stronger in our walk with Him and to develop a relationship of trusting in Him and not relying upon what we see! He puts us through processes to help us to grow, to be confident in who He is, to hear His voice, and to know it no matter how audible it is! God wants us to be able to declare who He is immediately, because He said My sheep know my voice, and a stranger they will not follow.

Faith is to a Christian as air is to breathe. We need it to survive. We will not see it all, no matter how bad we want to. We will not. We have got to learn to trust God, trust His plan, trust that He will never harm us, and never put more on us than we are able to bear! Allow your faith to get stronger by studying His Word and asking, what does God's Word have to say about this? Faith builds our spiritual fortitude! Our spiritual muscles! Once we have been strengthened, then we can strengthen our brothers and our sisters! The stronger we are in our Faith, the more God reveals to us the plan He has for our lives because He trusts us! How sweet it is to have God trust you! Like He trusted Job. He knew that no matter what the enemy threw at Job, Job would stay faithful. He would not be swayed.

Job stood steadfast because He knew who God was in his life! He knew what God had done, and they had a relationship! Going through the massive loss that Job experienced was no easy feat! But in the end, God gave Him double for all of his trouble because Job was trustworthy, and He trusted God! He didn't rely on what He saw, but what He knew and who He knew! That's where God wants us to be, and the only way we will get there is by having strong faith!

> *Job 13: 15-19 "So hold your tongue while I have my say, then I'll take whatever I have coming to me. Why do I go out on a limb like this and take my life into my hands? Because even if he killed me, I'd keep on hoping. I'd defend my innocence to the very end. Just wait; this is going to work out for the best—my salvation! If I were guilt-stricken, do you think I'd be doing this laying myself on the line before God?*
>
> **You'd better pay attention to what I'm telling you. Listen carefully with both ears. Now that I've laid out my defense, I'm sure that I'll be acquitted. Can anyone prove charges against me? I've said my piece. I rest my case.**

Faith keeps us grounded when everything else seems to be chaotic!

> *Colossians 2: 6-7 (NIV) So then, just as you received Christ Jesus as Lord, continue to live your lives in him, rooted and built up in him, strengthened in the faith as you were taught, and overflowing with thankfulness.*

Faith helps us make sense of the chaos. The vision that I get immediately when I think about this is when the disciples were on the ship, and the sea was tossing the boat in all kinds of ways and in every direction, and they looked upon the water, and the sea, whom they learned was Jesus, walking calmly on the water. Waves crashing all around Him, but He is walking calmly and unbothered! That is powerful! Or when He spoke to the storm and said, *Peace, be still,* and everything ceased and calmed under the sound of His command. That is what faith does for us when we believe and what is even more awesome is that Jesus instructed us to have faith the size of a mustard seed, and we can move mountains! Have you seen a mustard seed? It is like a little bigger than a poppy seed, and that is all the faith we need to move a MOUNTAIN!

My mom brought some mustard seeds and placed them in little plastic bags and taped them all over the house, where she would spend time, as a constant reminder of the size of the faith she is required to have! It was a great visual reminder! The world has seen a lot! The turmoil and the chaos from 1600 Pennsylvania Ave NW to the millions of lives lost due to COVID, but Jesus is still walking peacefully in the midst of the chaos. Knowing that God is still on the Throne is what gives us, as believers, the intestinal fortitude to hold on. Faith keeps us anchored when we want to go adrift! Faith keeps us focused on the One who is able to bring us through, while the media seeks to sensationalize world events, slant the truth, and depict the world in such a way that it doesn't seem redeemable.

It is our faith that keeps us in the midst of chaos when we hear another cancer diagnosis and another job lost! It is our faith that gives us the ability to walk through and carry on in the midst of injustices and the loss of innocent lives due to hatred. It is faith that we are able to stand, having done all that we could to stand. Our faith helps us to see that even though there are tragedies, there are still reasons to give God praise! Babies are still being born, and ventilators are being turned off as people begin to breathe on their own! Marriages are still taking place! Homes are being purchased! Innocent people that are incarcerated are being set free! Hope is springing up like a well of living water. If we just look and see! God is still in the blessing business! Faith helps us to see it, to embrace it, and to give God the praise, glory, and honor because as long as we have Faith in God, our life will continue to have meaning! Have no doubt, in the midst of chaos..... GOD IS STILL IN CONTROL!!

Faith is our anchor to which we hold steady when we want to drift away:

> *1 John 5:4-5, it says: "For everyone who has been born of God overcomes the world. And this is the victory that has overcome the world – our faith. Who is it that overcomes the world except for the one who believes that Jesus is the Son of God?" Yes, Jesus is our hope and anchor who will keep us in the midst of storms.*

Have you ever watched a palm tree during a storm? From a safe distance, of course! If you notice that a palm tree will sway and bend in whichever way the wind blows, it will not break! I have watched it thrash, twist, and turn with every blow, but once the wind stops, it reverts back to its same position. Its roots are so heavily grounded that it anchors it and holds it steady when the storms are raging! It is hard to uproot something or someone whose roots run deep!

What about a classic childhood toy called the "Weebles Wobble?" (I am truly dating myself now) Its catchphrase was "weebles, wobble, but they don't fall down!" You could hit it, kick it, push it, slam dunk it, whatever torment a child could inflict upon this toy, it took the hits and stood right back up! The creators of this toy were so clever, they put a smile on the toy's face, so when you hit it, it went down smiling and bounced back up smiling! Our faith keeps us grounded. Take your best shot and watch us get up, dust ourselves off, smile and say that's all you got? We do this because we wear the title of more than a conqueror!

We can be easily moved by what we see simply because we see it, and what we see has to be real, right? or so we think. It is easy to look at where we are and see the end of the story. Those nights when all we could do was cry ourselves to sleep, praying for the morning to come, or those days where it is a struggle just to get out of bed. We face a lot in life. That is why God, who has already walked out the steps in our life, told us to have faith in Him, not what we see. Have hope in Him, not in what the world can offer, because that is temporary, it is conditional, and it is fleeting!

The world has a way of snatching the proverbial rug from underneath us, catching us by surprise and leaving us shook. But we serve a God where nothing catches him by surprise! A God who knows our thoughts before we can think it! Who is there before us and remains after us! This is whom we need to have our faith rooted and grounded in!

> *I realize that sometimes in this life*
> *We're gonna be tossed by the waves*
> *And the currents that seem so fierce*
> *One thing I like*

But in the word of God, I've got an anchor, hallelujah
And it keeps me steadfast and unmovable
Despite the tide
But if the storms don't cease
And if the winds keep on blowing in my life
My soul has been anchored in the Lord
   —My Soul Has Been Anchored - Douglas Miller

Unexplainable Peace:

A Hole Where She Used To Be

A LETTER FROM MOM

Dear Mona, aka My Baby-girl

On December 17, 1969, at 5pm, it was a Wednesday in the Heart of Florida Hospital. You entered the world. I was 23 years old, unmarried, afraid, but I knew from the moment I laid eyes on you my life would take on an entirely new meaning. My blood pressure reached alarming heights, and I almost didn't make it as they attempted to lower my pressure, but God stepped in. At 6 months old, we followed your father's mother to Brooklyn, New York, and that is where I would raise you. Fresh from Philadelphia, I moved there to stay with my Aunt in order to pursue nursing school. I was used to city life, but I never thought this was where I would live and raise my baby girl.

ROMONA JACKSON

We started in Bed-Stuy, then moved to Crown Heights, and I watched you grow. I worked the 3 to 11 shift, so you were alone a lot of the time, but you were so smart. You learned at an early age how to care for yourself, how to fix yourself meals, and you gained an independence that I never had when I was younger. You never gave me any problems. You were a loner, quite like me, but when you did open up, your personality filled the room. I wanted to be for you, what I did not have. My mother passed away when she was 36 years old from breast cancer, and I did not know fully all that I needed to know, nor did I learn all that I needed to learn. I had to step up and help to raise my three sisters. It wasn't easy. I left home when my youngest sister was just a baby to pursue a nursing career that I never finished. I still regret leaving my baby sister to this day.

When I had you, I didn't know what love was. I didn't know how we were going to make it. All I knew was to work and take care of the home. The home wasn't a happy one. We had our share of more downs than we had ups, but all I wanted to do was make it good for you! I know you saw things that a young child should not have seen, heard things, and experienced things that probably to this day, you still recall, but when I look at you, I am amazed how you turned every bit of strife that you endured into a tool that helped to shape you and mold you into the woman that I stood in awe of watching. I wasn't the most affectionate mom. I remember you used to lay your head on my lap or attempt to, and I would push you away. It wasn't because I didn't love you. I just didn't know how to show you. I remember going through so many things when you were growing up that I sat and wrote you a letter that outlined everything that I wanted when I died because I felt like I wasn't going to be here for long. I told you the color

I wanted my dress to be, the gloves I wanted on my hands. You know they say hindsight is 20/20. Had I known better, I wouldn't have written you that letter because you were so young. It wasn't until you got older that I realized that it actually traumatized you. I planted a seed with that letter that caused a negative impact because you didn't want to leave my side. You were afraid to leave me, thinking you had to save me....I'm sorry, Mona.

You were my heart, and although I am no longer by your side, you still are. I am so proud of you! You were my best friend, and you lit up my life whenever you were around. I could talk to you, and you would see me. I could laugh with you and be me around you without a care in the world. When you told me you loved me, all of the love that I didn't receive was captured in all the words you would say to me. The time you spent with me. Even in our disagreements, my love for you never waned, I loved you unconditionally, and I tried my best to show you. To make up for the hugs that I didn't give, the kisses that I didn't share and I thank God for allowing me the opportunity to learn and grow through you! You were my unexpected teacher. I thought I taught you how to pray, but you taught me! You were more than my daughter. You were my best friend, and I thank God for helping me to fulfill my purpose, and that was to bring you into this world.

Now I watch, from the best seat in the house, what God is doing! Where distance stopped me when I was physically there, now I can be anywhere you are, at any time I want to be. I can watch you while you sleep, pray for you non-stop, I can be there when every tear falls and petition our Father to take the pain away. I can celebrate with you at every juncture and be right there with you. Can you feel me? Can you hear me? I sure hope so. I am so proud of you! My assignment didn't stop on October 24, 2020.

It only just began. My prayers for you didn't stop. They got even stronger. Mona, I knew I just couldn't tell you because there was a small part of me that wanted to stay, but if I did, you wouldn't be able to emerge from your cocoon and be that butterfly God showed me that you would be. I am thankful he allowed me to see your home and to see just a preview of what is to come. It gave me the peace that I needed, the peace in knowing you were going to be alright. That's why I sat in every part of your house. God's peace is there, Mona, and so am I. Oh yes, and those ducks, I asked God to send them so you can be reminded I am there watching over you.

So now, Mona, be who God called you to be without compromise! God is with you, and all that you need is within you! I know! I see it! Don't question who God made you! Take your time and trust God! Trust His Plan, Baby-girl, keep reading that picture I brought you. You know the one you have hanging on your wall. The one that says, "Beautiful Girl, you were made to do hard things, so believe in yourself!" I got your back! I got your front! Everything I taught you, from being a good woman to presenting yourself with class, style and dignity, do it! Live it! Be it! You are a winner! You are more than a conqueror! You are going to shake up the world! You are purpose fulfilled!

I know it hurts! It hurts me that I am not there with you, but you got this! You are God's child, and no good thing will He withhold from you! You always called me the epitome of the Proverbs 31 woman! Now, my Baby-girl, I call you the epitome of the Proverbs 31 woman, and don't you ever doubt. Live your life! Live your life! Live your life! If ever you find yourself doubting or when you need your head to be lifted, listen really close to your heart and hear me singing this to you!

You are my sunshine
My only sunshine
You make me happy when skies are gray
You'll never know just
How much I love you
Please don't take my Sunshine away

I love you, Baby-girl! Remember to do something good for yourself!

Love, Mommy

Trust that God knows how to heal the hurt. He knows how to fill the broken place where your loved one used to be. My heart has a hole the size and shape of my mom that I know will never be filled because only she can fill it, but I know God to be the mender of broken hearts. I would have never chosen this path, this curveball, this unexpected detour, but I have to trust God. I encourage you to do the same. When we declare the Words of Jeremiah 29:11, we shout it proudly because God has a plan, but sometimes we expect that it will always be smooth sailing, easy-riding. However, to get to where God wants you to be when you say YES to Him, it is going to take stretching, growing and being uncomfortable so we can be primed and pruned, pricked and prodded. We have to be crushed in order to get the oil, pressured to shine like diamonds, and placed in the fire so we can come forth as pure gold.

The process that God has we will never understand! Isaiah 55:8-9:

> *"For my thoughts are not your thoughts, neither are your ways my ways," declares the LORD. "As the heavens are higher than the earth, so are my ways higher than your ways and my thoughts than your thoughts.*

So we have to rest in the confidence that this is part of the plan that God has for me! It hurts, it doesn't feel good, but if you're reading this book and you have experienced a great loss, you have to trust God and know that He's got the plan, and within the plan, He has placed healing. There is something about being broken. When you are broken down spiritually, mentally, emotionally, and physically, you feel like there is nothing in this world that can help us or heal us. We start to ask why? We start doing things to take the pain away.

We look at all of the broken pieces that are scattered about, and we try to put ourselves back together, not realizing that God wants to add newness to our pieces, that the same pieces that fell off for a reason. We have to grow, and we have outgrown the broken pieces. They will no longer fit in the same socket because our sockets have changed because yet while broken....we grew.

> *Romans 8:28 And we know that all things work together for good to them that love God, to them who are the called according to his purpose.*
>
> *Romans 8:18 For I reckon that the sufferings of this present time are not worthy to be compared with the glory which shall be revealed in us*

The Word of God gives us life! We find in it everything we need to help us to endure! Cleave to it and hide it in your heart and recite it daily! It is the Word as you would eat physical food! The Bible tells us that we cannot live on bread alone, but by every word that proceeds out of the mouth of God shall we live! *(**Matthew 4:4**)* We need to be fed Spiritually and build upon the hope of Christ and rest upon His Promises. Watching my mom, I experienced an unexplainable peace, and I realize now it was the peace that God had promised. I watched my mom's health decline right before my eyes, but I had peace. I felt like I should have been screaming and yelling and pumping my fists at everyone, but instead, I had peace. The peace didn't take away the hurt, but it allowed me to remain calm, so I could hear Him clearly and manage.

We all experience things differently. We carry the weight of grief and hurt differently, but what remains constant, what remains consistent, is the One who can heal the hurt and put us back together again! The phenomenal Psalmist, Tramaine Hawkins, said it best through the words of this beautiful song,

> *"Ye who are broken stop by the Potter's House! Ye who need mending, stop by the Potter's House! Give Him the fragments of your broken life. My friend the Potter wants to put you back together again! Oh, the Potter wants to put you back together again!"*

We have to not be ashamed and come to God where we all are! Bring our "Holey" selves to Him so he can mend our holes! If we want unexplainable peace, we have to give our explainable chaos to Him and know He will soothe us! Prayer is our direct connection to Him, and no matter where we are, we can pray! It doesn't matter our posture. What matters is the position of our hearts! We have to come before the One who saw the hurt long before we knew it was coming and ask Him to heal! We try to carry things on our own, but we cannot! Do you know what the beautiful thing is? God is waiting for us with His outstretched arms, ready, willing, and able to give us just what we need. Press in!

The Journey Ends, Legacy Begins

"The memory of the righteous will be for a blessing...."
—Proverbs 10:7

Webster's Definition: Legacy ('le-gə-sē) something transmitted by or received from an ancestor or predecessor or from the past

Biblical definition: Legacy focuses on what will endure. It's about passing on things of lasting value to those who will live on after us. Legacy involves living intentionally and aiming to build into the next generations for their success.

When I look at the word legacy, I get this overwhelming sense of pride, joy, and strength, but I also feel the weight of responsibility that carrying on the memory or what someone has started is a huge responsibility and can be a daunting task but it can and should be done. I look at where we are right now, and in my opinion, someone stopped telling their story. What do I mean by that? I see a lot of history repeating itself, young people falling into traps that could have been avoided. Now let me add a disclaimer that sometimes they are told but still fall into the traps, but that is what I call a lesson that needs to be learned, hence enter the "school of hard knocks," but I will go back to my first point, we all go through things in life, we have experiences that we should be able to share with others and help them go another way.

Like the Mothers of the church that sit on the front pew and sweetly pull the young ladies aside, if their skirt is too short or too tight, they would place a handkerchief over your legs to cover your knees and hand you a piece of tissue so you can spit that gum out! They would teach the ladies etiquette, how to take care of a home and how to cook meals while teaching them to excel in school and get good grades. The Deacons would teach the young men how to be men, how to be handy with their hands, fix things around the house, teaching them how to take care of their mothers and grandmothers so they can subsequently know how to take care of their wives and daughters. I remember sitting and listening to my grandfather tell the story of how they came up and what they did not have, and how we should be appreciative. I remember walking away having a sense of pride in where I came from and the responsibility to be grateful and to carry on the forward progression.

Now we have mothers too young to have a history! Children are being raised on social media and being taught that having the latest Tik Tok move and the most likes define who you are and what you will be. We have single-headed households with no support, our "villages" are disappearing, and it is an "every man and woman for themselves" mentality. The church is losing its voice due to people not sharing the testimonies or forgetting where they came from and turning down their noses in judgment, causing people to not be able to tell the difference between the world and the church! They stopped telling the story!

Rich legacies are housed within the eternal home of the cemetery! Left untouched because we need more people who are willing to tell the story and fulfill the legacy, so the legacy doesn't stop when the person who began the movement transitions on… the legacy must continue. Legacy cannot just be defined as monetary, but it can be described as the intangible. If we knew our history, there would be greater pride in where we have come from! Greater work to preserve history! Greater tenacity to change what didn't work so we will not repeat what went wrong, thereby creating a perpetual cycle of dysfunction and negativity!

There is good news if we all decide to preserve the legacy within our families, one family at a time, communities will be changed and impacted in a masterful way because we have something to aspire to. We take on a good sense of responsibility to make sure that it doesn't die. The legacy of Carolyn Ruth White Jackson, born August 18, 1946, transitioned from labor to reward on October 24, 2020, will live on in me! I will pick up where she left off and carry forward as a part of my life what she worked so hard to achieve. My mother desired love and desired love to be in every aspect of her home! There was not a door to be closed because of anger or strife, but she welcomed everyone in her home and knew no strangers. She would encourage and give hope to those who felt like they did not have anyone or anything, and she made it a point to make everyone feel like someone and to feel loved without condition! She kept her home immaculate because she knew it was a representation of her and also a home where God would abide, and she always wanted there to be a sense of peace in the home! She wanted it to be a sanctuary, a safe haven!

My mother enjoyed laughter, and she loved to cook! She showed her love by way of pots and pans! Her love shined through each dish! That is what made her the phenomenal cook she was! My mother was, to some, a mother, a sister, and a friend that they never had! She was a woman of integrity! A woman of moral values! A woman of God! She loved the Lord with all that she had, and she did all that she could to live upright before Him! She wanted to make God proud because if she did that, then everything else would fall into place. Her legacy contained faith! She was a woman who believed and had that mustard seed faith! She trusted, and therefore she believed, and God granted her petitions! My goal is to be whom God has called me to be while continuing the legacy of my mother! She did not have a lot of money, but she was wealthy when it came down to love and how she showed it! I will carry forth that legacy, and by doing so, my mother will always live on through me!

LEGACY KEEPER!

What legacy are you looking to carry forth? What are you showing your family and friends? How are you breaking cycles and building a legacy that will remain long after you are gone? Write it down here, and let it be your start!

_____

_____

_____

_____

_____

_____

_____

_____

_____

_____

_____

We all have a legacy to fulfill, and the world will be an even greater place when we don't let the cemetery be the end of the story! Don't place a period where legacy should begin!

God bless the person who is reading this book and the decisions that they will make that will determine the legacy that they lead. God help them to line up with your perfect will and plan for their lives so they will position themselves to receive all that you have in store for them. Help them with their mindset so that it is positive and focused on you! Help them to desire the things that will help them to leave not just an inheritance for their children's children but will change the whole trajectory of their legacy. Let their legacy be built on the sure foundation of your Word, and let it be built with your Love. Help every generational curse be broken, no matter what it is! Break curses of poverty, illiteracy, brokenness, self-doubt, bitterness, and unforgiveness! God, break any and everything that will try to come and destroy their legacy. We uproot every weed, every tare, every unfruitful thing that will try to rear its ugly head and speak contrary to what your Word has promised! We speak life! We speak and declare a rich legacy has been birthed! We declare that their legacy will show all those to come to your Goodness, Your Kindness, Your Grace, and Your Favor! Thank you, God, for our blessed Legacy! In Jesus' Name! AMEN!

Praise God No Matter What

> *In this, you greatly rejoice, even though now for a little while, if necessary, you have been distressed by various trials, so that the proof of your faith, being more precious than gold which is perishable, even though tested by fire, may be found to result in praise and glory and honor at the revelation of Jesus Christ.*
> 1 Peter 1:6-7

I sat in mom's hospital bed, and she would just cry. I don't know about you, but the worst sound ever to me is the sound of my mother crying. I hated to hear her cry. I would do anything within my power to stop it. It broke my heart into a million pieces. When I heard her crying, I would jump up and ask mommy, why are you crying? What's wrong? Are you in pain? Do you need more medication? She would say no. But I didn't let it go. I pressed on, mommy, are you sure? What can I get you? She would say nothing, nothing at all! Kept asking her and asking her until it frustrated her, and then I would apologize and tell her, mommy, I just don't want to see you crying. Her response to me was Mona, I am crying because God is so good.

I would sit back in my chair in awe. She would begin to pray. My mother prayed non-stop during her illness, and it wasn't God, please heal me. It was God I love you! God, I thank you! God, you are so good! God, you are better than good. When the pain would come, it would get stronger! I love you, Lord! You don't make any mistakes! I praise you, God! I trust you, God! There is no one like you, God! I learned through this how-to praise God no matter what I was going through. One of the greatest lessons I learned by watching my mother! How to praise when you don't feel like praising! How to push through when you barely have the strength to breathe! I recall playing the gospel song by Helen Miller, Lean on me. My mom actually got a chance to see her minister that song in her home church, and to this day, it is hard for me to fully listen to that song, but I can picture my mother.

She was lying in bed, eyes full of water, and she started waving her hands while singing, *"I won't let you fall if you just lean on me."* Then it turned into a prayer! I know you won't let me fall! I know you won't let me fall, Jesus! Then we would sing Victory is mine! And her praise would get stronger! She could not remember a lot of things, but when those songs came on, she sang them word for word with such fervor it resonated throughout the entire room, and I could feel the Spirit enter in. Watching my mother do this made me repent for all the times I didn't praise because I didn't feel like it or because I didn't feel like pressing in. My mother taught me that no matter what she went through, she was going to praise God! Nothing broke her praise! Nothing broke her spirit! My mom knew that her healing was in her praise, and the more she praised, the more she would be healed. We just had to understand that it would be complete healing….just not on this side.

I don't know what you may be experiencing by the time this book reaches your hands and you decide to read, but I pray that you never lose your praise. The Joy of the Lord is the strength of His people (Nehemiah 8:10). When we focus on praise, it frees God to move without our feeble interruption. Whenever we read about praise within the scriptures, it was, in most cases, before the battle. Before they went to war, they sang, danced, and played tambourines. **(2 Chronicles 20:21)** Praise invoked the presence of the Lord. Praise was our weapon, the most powerful tool that we carry in our arsenal! Praising God for who He is and giving Him praise in advance shows God that we know what He is able to do! We know that we are already victorious so let me praise you in advance! Just like I watched my mom do! She wasn't healed, but she praised Him! Her body still experienced great pain, but she still praised Him! She couldn't walk anymore without pain! But she found it still within her to give Him praise. Whether she was healed on this side or healed on the other side, my Mother deemed God worthy to be praised!

Revelations 4:11 says that we were created to give God worship, so when we praise Him despite the circumstance, we are fulfilling the purpose to which we were created! Before Daniel fought the Giant, He began to boast about God and who He was! He began to give honor, praise, glory, and reverence to God! This caused God to move on His behalf! He heard the boasting and the praise. He heard the sheer belief that He had in Him. Therefore, God had to move! He had to grant His request! (**1 Samuel 17:34-49**) Our praise moves GOD!

> *Praise keeps us connected to God! Psalm 33:1 Sing joyfully to the Lord, you righteous; it is fitting for the upright to praise him. (NIV)*

Praising God is our love language to God. It is how we stay focused and centered on Him and who He is in our lives! It keeps us humble knowing that everything that we have, everything that we hoped for, Everything that we are, and everything that we hope to be lies in Him, and if He does not release it, it shall not be done! Praise keeps us God-centered and God-focused!

> *Praise helps us to bask in His Omnipresence! Psalm 22:3 But thou art holy, O thou that inhabitest the praises of Israel. (KJV)*

Have you ever been in your house, cleaning to your favorite gospel playlist, and then you found yourself flat on your face in worship! God is omnipresent, meaning, He is everywhere at the same time! Because He inhabits, lives in, our praise whenever we praise Him, He allows us to feel Him making us aware of His Presence! He lives in true praise and worship!

> *Praise replaces worry! Jeremiah 17:7 But blessed is the one who trusts in the Lord, whose confidence is in him, (KJV).*

We have all heard if you are going to pray, then don't worry, but if you are going to worry, then don't pray! You cannot worry and pray at the same time. It is like oil and water, it just doesn't mix! The same with praise! We can replace "pray" with "praise," and it will carry the same meaning! When we praise God, we are showing an outward reflection of our inward belief that he is going to do just what He said, and the more we praise, the more we believe, because we start replaying over and over in our minds the things that God has already done! The things he has brought us through, and we start to build our praise because we know that what He has done before surely, without question, He will do it again. So our praise reinforces our confidence in God and His ability to do what only He can do!

Praise Keeps us humble under His Mighty Hand! 1 Corinthians 15:10a But by the grace of God, I am what I am!

Without God, I can do nothing! Without God, I would fail! Without God, my life would be drifting like a ship without a sail! These words are echoing within my spirit! They are a constant reminder that God is the source of my entire being, and I can do nothing without Him, and with that, it keeps me humble! Every resource that I have! Every strategy that I devise! Every word of wisdom that I am able to speak and every table that I am afforded to take a seat at is because God has deemed it possible. So when we praise, it reminds us of who God is, and it puts our infinite mind in perspective of his finite mind and overcomes it with humility! The more we praise God, the more aware we become of His Omnipotence! The more our frailty comes to view! We praise God because He is God!

Praise God no matter what! I believe that at this juncture in my life, I have endured the greatest hurt I could ever imagine, and I praise God in advance for His healing! I thank God in advance for what he will do and has already done! I thank Him for walking out the steps in my life, including these steps that were the hardest for me to pick my feet up and put them down in! He knew, and it was a part of His Plan! Don't let doubt, fear, bitterness, or any other negative trait extinguish your praise! The more you praise, the more you will heal, the more He will fill within you, and the more you will be able to share with others!

No matter what the day may bring to you
Keep praising God!
Whether up or down
Good or bad
Keep your praise always
    —Fred Hammond—Keep on Praising'

REFLECT AND GIVE THANKS SELF CHECK

Write down some things you are thankful for.

_____

_____

How will you keep your praise going?

_____

_____

I will bless the Lord at all times, and His praise shall continually be in my mouth! (Psalm 34:1)

God, for you alone, is worthy to receive Glory, Honor, and Praise! Lord, we bless you right now for all the things you have done and for all of the things that you will continue to do! Thank you for moving, and thank you for showing yourself strong in each and every one of us! You are our Father. You are our Keeper! You are our Deliverer, and there is NO ONE like you! We give you all the worship and praise that you are so deserving of! We bless you, God, for every word that shall be received from the pages of this book! We praise you for the healing that will come, the changes that will take place, all to make us better servants within your Kingdom! You are an awesome God, and we give you thanks! In Jesus' Name, we Bless you continually!!! AMEN

ROMONA JACKSON

VISION OF BEAUTY

JUST TO KNOW US! BEST FRIENDS FOREVER

ROMONA JACKSON

KEEP YOUR PRAISE ALWAYS! SMILING THROUGH THE PAIN

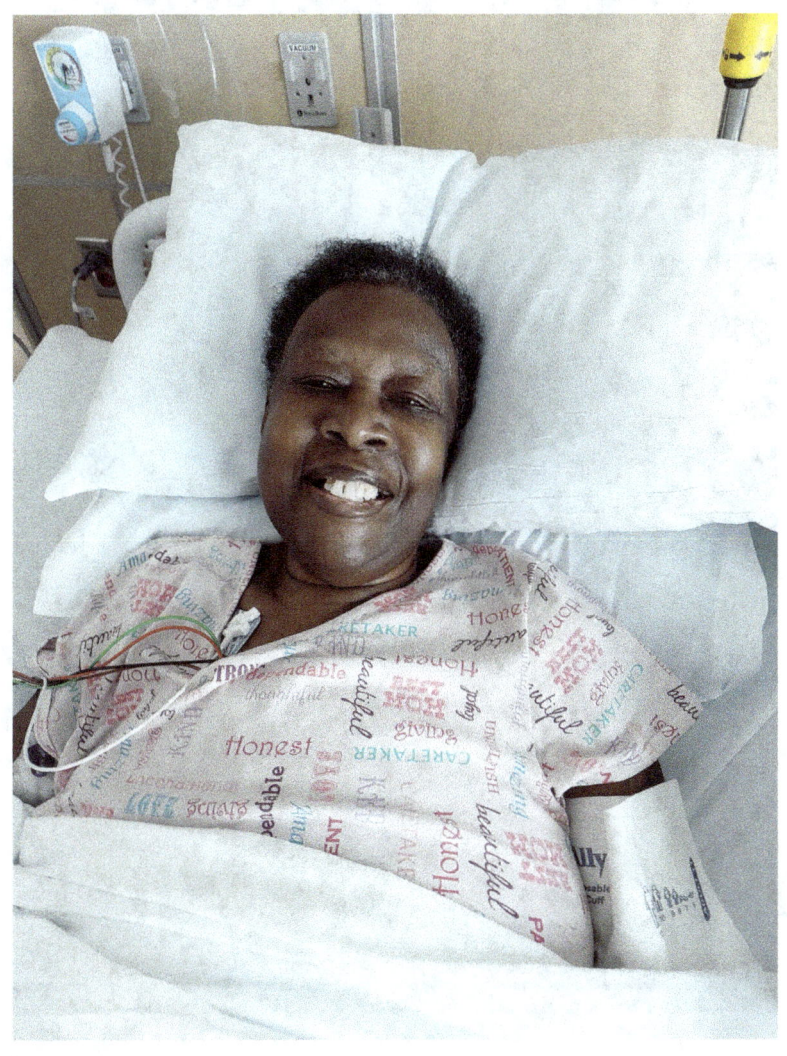

SHE LOVED HER TATTOOS

ROMONA JACKSON

NEVER GOODBYE...
JUST SEE YOU LATER!

What are your Takeaways, and What Will you Share! I would love to know! Please share what impacted you the most after reading this book. List three takeaways and three things you will share to help spread the message! Please post on any one of my social media platforms below or email me.

I was impacted most by:

_____

_____

My Three Takeaways are:

1. _____

   _____

2. _____

   _____

3. _____

   _____

I am going to share:

1. _____

   _____

2. _____

   _____

3. _____

   _____

Proverbs 3: 4-6 (The Message)

Earn a reputation for living well in God's eyes and the eyes of the people. Trust God from the bottom of your heart; don't try to figure out everything on your own. Listen for God's voice in everything you do, everywhere you go; he's the one who will keep you on track.

Acknowledgments

There are so many people that I can thank for being not just in my circle but in my corner during these past difficulties. I had people come and pray, text, and call just to let me know they were in my corner. Friends who had experienced the same type of loss who just wanted to let me know, in their small way, that I was not alone. Like my fraternity brother of Phi Beta Sigma Fraternity, Incorporated, Landry A. Johnson. I walked on the campus of Florida A&M University in 1992 alone and did not know how to navigate. When we met, I told him I felt like all my protection was gone and I had no one. He remembered these words and became the brother who looked out for his sister, and I will never forget that! He took the time during my loss to make thank you cards adorned with my mother's picture and beautiful words of sentiments because he wanted me to know he was there to support his sister. He will never know the impact that made on my life. He will always be my brother for who I am grateful to have.

There were also two families that stood out the most that I must mention, and that is Deacon Reggie and Deaconess Tammy

Wilson and their beautiful daughter, Artavia, who I coined my "Butterfly," and Deacon George and Deaconess Annette Kleckley. These two families embraced me like never before. They took off work to travel with me, without blinking an eye! They sat in my home and, in some cases, stayed the night at my house. They sat on the phone with me when I traveled down the highways to make sure I didn't fall asleep on the road and deposited money in my account to make sure I had gas and food while traveling. They sent text messages that greeted me at the perfect time, and even more so when all the other phone calls, messages, and visits stopped, they remained, and that is priceless.

I also want to acknowledge Jakyia and RJ. They stayed at my home for weeks to make sure I wasn't alone. Oftentimes, they just sat in silence, allowing me to grieve, and then did what they could to help me through! It may not seem like a lot to some, but to me, during the time when my world stopped spinning on its axis, these people held me up, and I will be forever grateful to each, and every one of them, and I pray that God will richly bless them and pour back into their lives in the same manner to rich they unselfishly poured out into mine!

About the Author

A native of Brooklyn, New York, and a proud graduate of Florida A&M University located in Tallahassee, Florida. She graduated from this historical institution with a degree majoring in Broadcast Journalism. Romona has a background in radio, where she worked as Program Director for WAMF-90.5, hosted her own Gospel radio morning show, and served as Mistress of Ceremony for a host of events.

Romona gained experience and served her community as a Regional Banking District Manager for Wells Fargo, overseeing the operation of the Gainesville District, which comprises eight branches and one-hundred and four team members, and is now transitioning as an entrepreneur! Launching FinanSense, LLC, Romona will serve as a financial coach with a focus on helping to educate and empower individuals, families, ministries, and organizations on money management and strengthening their overall financial plan and outlook through one on one coaching sessions and financial literacy workshops!

She is also the owner of Total Life Productions, LLC, where she earns credit as an author by having published two books: **Redefining Me: A 90 Day Devotional** and **Know Your Worth: You Are Not Your Past.** With the upcoming release of her third book: **Crazy Faith, Unexplainable Peace: Lessons My Mother Taught Me.** As a Playwright, Romona has produced and debuted two stage-plays, *"Train up a Child"* and *"Me, Myself and God,"* and has directed two plays for the Star Center Theater: **Aretha** and **The Bodyguard,** where she has the distinct privilege of serving as the President of the Star Center Executive Board.

Because of her life experiences, Romona is passionate about helping to rejuvenate and energize individuals and families holistically, striving to help build strong families, thereby resulting in strong communities spiritually, physically, and financially. Romona is a motivational speaker, a certified financial coach, a certified Zumba instructor, a certified Les Mills BodyPump instructor, and an avid runner. She is also a dedicated member of Faith Church, a proud member of Zeta Phi Beta Sorority, Incorporated, for 27 years and an excited member of the Gainesville Chapter (FL) of The Links, Incorporated.

MY BUTTERFLY

Every day I see a butterfly as it flies by so gracefully. So graceful, so beautiful, so vibrant and full of colors, and so much life. Every now and then, one would fly directly in front of me and stand still as if to greet me and say hello. It would follow me for a little while and then fly away as if to say see you later. You always said, after my Aunt, your sister, transitioned to her Heavenly home, to always say "see you later" instead of "Goodbye." Goodbye means forever but "see you later," says that we will meet again.

So I will say see you later, mommy and never say goodbye because I know if I live right, I will see you again! So until then, I will embrace and cherish every butterfly that comes my way and sees it as you stopping by to say I am free, I have no pain, so you don't have to worry about me. I am with my Father, which is the best place to be. So smile, Baby girl! I am always with you! It's never, ever goodbye but always see you later!

CONTACT THE AUTHOR

Facebook: https://www.facebook.com/RomonaJacksonRedefined

Facebook: https://www.facebook.com/knowyourworth2019

Instagram: @romonajackson_redefined

Email: contact@romonajackson.com

Website: https://www.romonajackson.com